OH MY GRANDFATHER

Stephen Chifunyise

Booklove Publishers

BOOKLOVE PUBLISHERS
P O Box 1917, Gweru, Zimbabwe
E-mail: booklove87@yahoo.com
Website: www.booklovepublishers.co.zw

OH MY GRANDFATHER

First published 2018

Editor: E A Makadho
Assistant Editors: Agari Vambe
                   Nomsa Chirisa

ISBN: 978 0 7974 7362 1

Published in Zimbabwe
by Booklove Publishers
printed by Serveplus Investments
2018

CONTENTS

DEDICATION

To my late wife Tisa Mwape Chifunyise.

CHARACTERS IN THE PLAY

Joseph Matanga: A senior civil servant in his early sixties. Fatherly, very protective and loving husband.

Monica Matanga: Joseph's loving wife. A motherly educator, committed to her preschool business.

Dorcas Matanga: Sixteen-year-old daughter of Joseph and Monica. Very aggressive feminist.

Morgan Matanga: Fourteen-year-old son of Joseph and Monica. He is a disciplined and respectful young man who is eager to learn.

Mutumwa Matanga: Eighty-year-old father of Joseph Matanga. A peasant farmer. A wise man who reads a lot about the history of his people and country. He respects his culture and is sensitive to other people's views and opinions.

Tendai Matanga: Joseph Matanga's younger sister. A mother of two who works as a security guard at a departmental store. Very close to her brother's family. A feminist and a woman empowerment promoter who respects her traditions but questions them.

Maidei Chitaka: Maid in the Matanga household. A very obedient, trustworthy and hardworking woman, married and a mother of three.

Johannes Mutero: A gardener at the Matanga house-hold: A 50-year-old man.

SETTING OF THE PLAY

The play is set in the Matanga living room, in the suburb of Borrowdale West, in Harare. It is a well-furnished room which shows that the family is well-to-do. On a huge table are a big television set, a DVD player and a music system. Next to the table is a bookshelf with books, magazines, newspapers, decorative crafts, sculptures of animals and people and small clay pots. There are fancy sofas. In between the sofas are small coffee tables. All the furniture stands on a multi-coloured carpet. On the walls of the room are photos of the Matanga family, namely Joseph Matanga (father), Monica Matanga (mother), Dorcas Matanga (daughter) and Morgan Matanga (son).

PART ONE

(Morgan enters. He is dressed in a fancy tracksuit and fancy trainers. He picks up a CD from a pile of CDs on top of a DVD player, places it into the music system, increases the volume and then comes to the centre of the room and begins to dance to music. He performs a complicated dance routine. Stops and claps his hands with the satisfaction that he has completed a complicated dance routine. He takes out a cellphone from the pocket of his tracksuit top, punches a number and waits expectantly.)

Morgan: *(shouts excitedly).* Coach! I got it. I have completed your complicated dance routine without a single error. I am meticulous and great. *(He laughs joyously.)* Please put me in the front row. I am going to make you and myself proud. I am exercising every morning and evening. I want to be very fit and smooth. Girls will scream when I take off my shirt at the end of the dance routine. *(He laughs then listens with a big smile that breaks into shrill joyful laughter.)* Thank you coach for your choreography. If Michael Jackson was still alive I would have recommended you to become his chief choreographer. *(He laughs then switches off the cellphone, puts it back into the pocket and begins the dance routine again, this time counting the movements loudly.)*

(Maidei, the housemaid, enters. She is dressed in a very smart housemaid's uniform. She is carrying a bundle of newspapers

*and magazines. She dumps the items near the music system,
then lowers the volume of the music. Morgan stops dancing and
screams.)*

Morgan: *(screaming).* Why? *(Confronting Maidei.)* Why Sisi?
Why did you do that?

Maidei: Do what, Morgan?

Morgan: Why did you do that to my music? I can't hear anything.

Maidei: With that noise, I can't hear anything from the radio.

Morgan: You are in the kitchen, Sisi! You are listening to a radio
in the kitchen. I am practising a very sophisticated
choreography for the national *Jibilika* hip-hop
championships. I can't dance without hearing the
music. I have to feel the music in the bones in every
part of my body.

Maidei: I can't hear anything from the radio with your music
shaking my heart and blocking my ears.

Morgan: Look, Sisi. I need just one hour to practise my dance
sequence. If you cannot stand loud music, why don't
you block your ears with cotton wool or a dish towel?
*(He goes to the music system and increases the
volume of the music. Maidei shakes her head and
walks out. Morgan does some complicated and
physically demanding movements which end with him
lying on the floor on his stomach. There is a loud knock
at the door of the main entrance. Morgan stands up,*

goes to the music system and switches off the system. He shouts loudly.) Come in! *(He goes towards the main entrance. When no one enters, he shouts again.)* Come in! *(He goes closer and finds Mutumwa Matanga, his grandfather, standing at the entrance. Matanga is dressed in an old black suit, a white shirt, a black tie, black shoes and a black hat. He is carrying a suitcase in his left hand and has a walking stick in his right hand. Morgan shouts excitedly.)* Hey, it's you, grandfather!

Mutumwa: *(with a big smile).* Yes, it is me, Muzukuru Dzingai!

Morgan: *(with wild, expressive gestures).* Come right in, Grandfather! *(Morgan walks to a sofa. Mutumwa puts down his suitcase on a spot at the entrance inside the room, walks to a sofa and sits down.)* Welcome, Grandfather! *(Mutumwa does not respond but continues looking at his suitcase. Morgan sits down near his grandfather.)* So how are you, Grandfather?

Mutumwa: Dzingai *muzukuru,* you are greeting me when my suitcase is at the entrance of your house. What welcome are you talking about?

Morgan: *(surprised and standing up).* Oh, Grandfather! I see what you mean. I am sorry! Absolutely sorry! *(He rushes to the entrance, grabs the suitcase, brings it and places it on a spot in front of his grandfather. Mutumwa looks at Morgan, picks up his walking stick and grabs the suitcase and begins to walk out. Morgan shouts.)* Grandfather, you are going away already? *(Mutumwa stops, turns around and laughs.)*

Mutumwa: Muzukuru. I have come to visit you in your home, here in Borrowdale. If you place my suitcase in front of me, it means that you have not welcomed me into your home.

Morgan: *(with an exaggerated gesture and hitting his head with both hands).* Oh, I see what you mean, Grandfather. It makes a lot of sense *(He rushes to his grandfather and extends a left hand to get the suitcase. Mutumwa uses his walking stick to push away Morgan's hand from his suitcase.)*

Mutumwa: *(instructively).* You want to take this suitcase from me with your left hand?

Morgan: I am terribly sorry again, Grandfather. *(He takes the suitcase with his right hand and begins to walk back into the room.)*

Grandfather: *(uses his walking stick to stop him and speaks instructively).* You should have taken my suitcase to your room or your parents' bedroom.

Morgan: I am sorry, Grandfather. You must have thought that I was telling you to go away from our home.

Mutumwa: That is why I took my suitcase and began going back to my home in Gutu.

Morgan: I am sorry, Grandfather. I do not know some of these things. In the past, every time you came to see us I was away at the boarding school. The only time I've been with you for any length of time was when we came over to you in Gutu at funerals and weddings. Unfortunately for me Grandfather, you were always busy with adult things and the cultural complications. So we never got to spend time together, really. I've had no time with you to learn things from you, Grandfather. I am very sorry for being so ignorant of what should be done.

Mutumwa: It is alright, Shumba. I shall teach you all you need to know about our way of doing things. After all, it is you who is to transmit our ways of doing things to the future generation. *(With a pleasant smile.)* Now, Muzukuru, please take my suitcase and walking stick to your room, then come back and greet me properly before you ask me how I am!

Morgan: Thank you, Grandfather. *(He extends his left hand to receive the suitcase from his grandfather. Mutumwa uses his walking stick to hit Morgan's hand. Morgan is shocked. He shakes his left hand showing pain and stares at his grandfather questioningly.)*

Mutumwa: *(angrily).* You do not receive anything from me or anyone with your left hand. To begin with, you do not give or receive anything from an elder with a left hand. Secondly, you do not receive anything from me or any elder with one hand.

Morgan: *(still shaking his left hand)*. I am sorry, I will not do that again. It seems I have a lot to learn, Grandfather.

Mutumwa: You tell me that you do not know what I have just said, Shumba?

Morgan: Honestly, I do not remember clearly anyone telling me not to use my left hand or one hand to receive things from elders. My dad and mum are not particular about these things.

Mutumwa: What? I can't believe that. *(Angrily.)* I am particular about that and many adults are particular about such things! It means there is a lot you do not know about our way of doing things. Now get the suitcase first. *(Morgan gets the suitcase with both hands.)* Now put it down and come and get the walking stick. *(Morgan puts down the suitcase and receives the walking stick with both hands.)* Good! *(Morgan picks up the suitcase and walks out. Mutumwa sits down on the same sofa, looks around, then sits up and begins to clap hands.)* Thank you, Shumba! Thank you, Sipambi! Thank you, Charumbira, *va*Nhinhi *vari* Nhinhihuru.[1] Thank you my ancestors for receiving my prayers and for asking Musikavanhu to guide me safely from Gutu to Harare. May you guide my stay here to be fruitful to my children and grandchildren? May what I say be what you expect me to instruct this generation with the wisdom handed down from generation to generation

---

1. The tough ones who lie buried at the place of the tough one.

by our founding ancestors? *Maita* Shumba. *(He claps hands, stops and sits back on the sofa. Morgan enters. He is now dressed in a multi-coloured shirt and the same pair of track suit trousers. He sits down on the sofa near his grandfather.)*

Morgan: So, how are you, Grandfather?

Mutumwa: *(laughs. Morgan is surprised)*. Shumba, you have not greeted me.

Morgan: Oh! I am sorry, Grandfather. *(He stands up, positions himself in front of his grandfather and extends his right hand for a hand shake. Mutumwa laughs even louder. Morgan is confused.)*

Mutumwa: Muzukuru, do you realise that you are looking down on me.

Morgan: Yes. I realise that.

Mutumwa: Why?

Morgan: Because I am standing up and you are seated.

Mutumwa: You are looking at the centre of my head! *(He touches the centre of his head.)* You are looking there, the centre of my head, aren't you?

Morgan: Yes. I am looking at the centre of your head.

Mutumwa: You see why you should not greet me while standing up and while I am seated? Only those who are older than you can afford to look down on you and gaze on the top of your head.

Morgan: Oh, I see! So that is why I should crouch when greeting you?

Mutumwa: Yes. *(Morgan goes down on his haunches and extends his right hand for the hand shake. Mutumwa grabs it and shakes his hand enthusiastically and happily.)* You should say, "*Mhoroi*" as we shake hands!

Morgan: *Mhoroi,* Grandfather!

Mutumwa: *Mhoro,* Muzukuru! *(They shake hands again. Morgan stands up and takes a seat in the sofa directly opposite where Mutumwa is sitting.)* Muzukuru, just call me Sekuru. I am not comfortable being called Grandfather even when we speak in English.

Morgan: Ok, Sekuru. I shall remember that. My Shona is not good, Sekuru.

Mutumwa: Why, Muzukuru? Shona is your language, your mother tongue. You started hearing Shona when you were in your mother's womb.

Morgan: *(laughing).* Come on, Sekuru. Babies inside their mothers' wombs cannot hear anything said outside their mother's womb. It is scientifically not possible. I mean biologically not possible.

Mutumwa: Your mother spoke to you when you were in her womb. Are you saying that she was crazy? *(Morgan laughs.)* When you were born the language your ears first heard was Shona, your mother's language. When I came to see you and your mother at Parirenyatwa Hospital, I held you in my arms and spoke to you in Shona. I said, *"Maita Shumba. Maita Sipambi. Uyu ndiye Dzingai. Ndamupa zita renyu Sipambi!"*[2] *(He claps his hands. Morgan joins him but claps his hands like a woman.)* Stop clapping your hands like that, Dzingai! You are not a woman! Men do not clap their hands like that!

Morgan: *(apologetic).* I am sorry, Sekuru. I normally do not do this traditional thing of thanking by clapping hands.

(Mutumwa laughs, expressing surprise. Maidei enters and kneels down in front of Mutumwa and holds her right hand with her left hand. With a big smile, she extends the hand to Mutumwa in greeting.)

Maidei: *Mhoroi, Sekuru!*

Mutumwa: *Mhoro, Muzukuru!*

Maidei: *(stands up and goes to sit on a sofa near Mutumwa).* I am sorry for not being here to welcome you when you arrived. I was at the back of the house collecting the laundry.

Mutumwa: Do not worry, Muzukuru. Dzingai welcomed me here very well.

Maidei: Thank you, Morgan. *(She turns to Mutumwa.)* How are you, Shumba?

---

2. Thank you, Lion. Thank you, Sipambi. This is Dzingai. I have given him your name, Sipambi.

Mutumwa: I am very well. How are you, Soko?

Maidei: I am very well, Sekuru. How are they at home?

Mutumwa: They are all well. How is your family in Gokwe?

Maidei: My family is well. Did you travel well?

Mutumwa: I travelled well, Muzukuru. By the way, your husband's totem is Hungwe, the fish eagle. Isn't it?

Maidei: Yes, Sekuru. It is Hungwe.

Mutumwa: Chasura, eh!

Maidei: *(laughing).* Yes. We say *(Clapping hands.) Shiri Maokomavi, zienda nomudenga. Maita mwana waChasura!*[3] *(Morgan laughs. Mutumwa and Maidei laugh too.)*

Morgan: *(laughing).* Sekuru, that is a naughty totem! Sounds like an insult.

Mutumwa: It sounds insulting, but it is someone's totemic praise. Insulting does not come into it. *Chasura upata uzere rusudzo. (He laughs. Maidei joins in laughing.)*

Maidei: Sekuru, let me go and make you tea.

Mutumwa: Good. The blend that I like, of course.

Maidei: *(standing up).* Yes, your favourite one Sekuru. We keep it just for you, Sekuru! Everyone here drinks coffee.

---

3. The bird of big claws. The ones who fly at the top of the sky. You have done well, child of the bird that farts. It has released a thunderous fart.

Mutumwa: Thank you for always having it there for me. *(As if advertising.)* My tasty tea, older than our independence!

Maidei: *(laughing and responding and advertising).* It lifts you up! Up! Up! And you become wide awake!

Mutumwa: *(clapping hands).* Thank you, *Mukanya. Vene voushe. Hekani Makwiramiti. Magaramugomo.*[4]

Maidei: Thank you, Shumba. *Maita Sipambi yakapamba nedzavamwe.*[5] *(Maidei and Mutumwa laugh together.)*

Mutumwa: Muzukuru. Bring me my tea at six o'clock. Right now, I need to sleep and rest just a little, for just one hour.

Maidei: Alright, Sekuru, I will bring your tea at six o'clock. Tea to lift you up! Up! Up! *(She laughs. Mutumwa joins in the laughing. Maidei exits to the kitchen, leaving Mutumwa laughing.)*

Morgan: *(curiously).* Sekuru, why does Sisi Maidei call you Sekuru when she is not your son's daughter or your daughter's daughter?

Mutumwa: Her mother's totem is Shumba, Lion, my totem, your totem. Therefore, I am her mother's brother, her uncle. You, too, are her uncle.

Morgan: Are you saying that anyone who is of the lion totem is my relation, my brother or my sister?

---

4. Monkey. The rulers. Behold, the tree climbers. Those who live in the mountains.
5. Thank you, Lion, the one who grabbed other people's property.

Mutumwa: Your big father, *babamukuru*, or your young father, *babamunini*. They could be Shumba Sipambi like us. They could be Shumba Mhazi, Shumba Nyamuziwa, Shumba Murambwi, Shumba Jichidza or Shumba Gurundoro.

Morgan: All those lions, Sekuru. This totem thing is very complicated and confusing.

Mutumwa: Complicated? What do you mean by that?

Morgan: How am I expected to know about Shumba Sipambi, Shumba Mhazi, Shumba Gurundoro, Shumba eh...?

Mutumwa: Give me answers to the following questions quickly. *(Shouts quickly like a teacher challenging students in a class.)* Seven times two!

Morgan: Fourteen!

Mutumwa: Twenty minus five!

Morgan: Fifteen!

Mutumwa: Thirty divided by ten!

Morgan: Three!

Mutumwa: Twenty five plus twenty five!

Morgan: Fifty!

(Mutumwa claps his hands. Morgan smiles with satisfaction.)

Mutumwa: Do you know something about the Second World War?

Morgan: Yes, Sekuru. Even about the First World War.

Mutumwa: Which people were responsible for causing that war?

Morgan: The Germans.

Mutumwa: How come you know about the First and Second World Wars and about the Germans?

Morgan: Sekuru, we are taught that as History. It is a subject in which we are examined. It is in textbooks.

Mutumwa: How come you were able to answer my arithmetic questions?

Morgan: Sekuru, I started learning arithmetic from Grade One.

Mutumwa: Our totems are an important part of our history, an important part of our identity. Our totems must be known by all of you.

Morgan: Nobody teaches us that history or that identity, Sekuru. No one has taught me about Shumba Sipambi or any other Shumba. Even when we were at the village in Gutu, none of the young people called each other Shumba. Only elders called each other Shumba.

Mutumwa: Why did you not ask why the elders were calling each other Shumba and you did not?

Morgan: When I asked one of the boys whether his surname was Mhofu, the name you used to call his father, the boy laughed at me.

Mutumwa: You did not ask questions because you feared that people would laugh at you?

Morgan: Yes.

Mutumwa: Let me tell you something for nothing. Never fear to be laughed at. Ask and you will be made to know what you do not know. Ask me any question and, if I know the answer, I will tell you. If I do not know, I will tell you that I do not know.

Morgan: Are you not going to say: "Ah, Muzukuru, how can you not know that?"

Mutumwa: *(laughing).* No, Dzingai. I will not do that. I do not expect you to know everything. I will also ask you questions about things I do not know. There is a lot you know which I do not know.

Morgan: *(urgently and in a very alert manner).* Are you serious about that, Sekuru? I know a lot you do not know?

Mutumwa: Yes, Muzukuru. You should also be my teacher. Learning does not end.

Morgan: *(laughs).* By the way, Sekuru, I am no longer called Dzingai but Morgan.

Mutumwa: What?

Morgan: *(impatiently).* I was baptised three months ago. I had to change the name because our pastor, Prophet Zindonga, said that Dzingai was not a good name and that…

Mutumwa: A prophet called Zindoga said that the name I gave you was not a good name?

Morgan: Yes. Prophet Zindoga of our new church, The Wealth Creation Ministry of Christ.

Mutumwa: Your prophet pastor of the Ministry of Wealth Creation said that my name was not a good name?

Morgan: You see, Sekuru. Dzingai means eh... eh.. eh...ehhh!

Mutumwa: *(harshly).* Chase! Chase away! Get rid of!

Morgan: *(excitedly).* You see what I mean, Sekuru? Chase away! Chase away what? How can anyone be called Chase Away?

Mutumwa: *(laughs pointing a finger at him in disbelief. Morgan stares at his grandfather confused).* I was given that name Dzingai by my father to remind our family what people did to him. *(Very animated.)* Your father may not have explained anything about your name. Now, let me tell you. It is going to be a very long explanation. Do not get tired of listening.

Morgan: No, Sekuru. I will not be tired of listening to you. Go ahead. Explain, Sekuru.

Mutumwa: *(as if storytelling)*. My father came to Gutu from Shurugwi just after the First World War! My father was a medicine man - a doctor and a hunter. After marrying my mother, a jealous man called Zirema, who also wanted to marry my mother, spread a lie - a dangerous lie that my father was a sorcerer – *muroyi!* He convinced many villagers that my father should be chased away from Zongororo village. My mother pleaded with the headman *(Imitating and acting out and clapping hands.)* "Mhukahuru! Samanyanga! Matyoramiti![6] I plead with you. I speak the truth. I speak on the name of my mother, your sister, who lies at Dembetembe. My husband is a very good man. He is a wise and kind man! He is a good medicine man. He is not a sorcerer!" But the rest of the people of Zongororo shouted. "Chase him away! Chase him! He is bad!" While the villagers were shouting and demanding that my father be chased away, the elder son of headman Zongororo who had been beaten by a snake was brought to them by his brothers. Fortunately, the boys had killed the snake that had beaten the boy. My father examined the dead snake and the snake bite. He requested that he be allowed to go to the bush to get medicine to treat the snake bite. The headman allowed my father to go for the medicine. My father took a knife and put it close to a hot flame, then cut a small wound at the point of the snake bite on the boy's leg. He squeezed out some blood. He told the boy to hold the wound to stop more bleeding then ran very fast to the forest. A short while

---

6.   The great animal! The horned one! The breaker of trees!

16

later, my father came back breathing hard. He came with a bark of a certain tree. He took fibre from the bark and put it into a mortar. He pounded the fibre and squeezed the sap into the wound he had cut. The boy screamed with pain saying, *"Maiwe-e!"*[7] My father squeezed more sap into the wound. The boy screamed again *"Maiwe-e!"* and collapsed. The villagers thought the boy was dead but my father smiled and shouted, "Don't worry! He is alright!" He opened the boy's mouth and squeezed some drops of the sap into the mouth. The boy woke up. My father took the fibre and squeezed out the sap and tied the fibre around the snake-bite wound. Headman Zongororo and all the villagers who wanted my father chased away from Zongororo were delighted. Headman Zongororo shouted, "Matanga is a good man! He is our doctor! Matanga shall not leave our village. *Maita* Shumba. *Maita* Sipambi." Every one shouted, "Matanga is our doctor!" My parents did not leave Zongororo village. When I was born, my father named me Dzingai, "chase away!" to remind our family about that story - the story of my father. The story of our family. You are now the custodian of that story of our family. Dzingai! Names are special gifts. They are a heritage - a very important asset you should not throw away just like that. You are now the custodian of our heritage.

---

7.   Oh, my mother, my mother!

Morgan: *(claps hands excitedly as if an applause to a performance)*. That is a fantastic story, Sekuru. Fabulous story. Incredible story. Your father was a hero! A great doctor! I need to write down that story properly, Sekuru. I need to write our family tree, your father's father and his father's father and all before them. I need to record all the great things our family has done.

Mutumwa: *(excitedly)*. I will tell you everything, Muzukuru. You will write down the whole history of our family. You will write what happened in Shurugwi, in Gutu and in Chivi.

Morgan: Sekuru, you mean our family lived in Shurugwi and Chivi?

Mutumwa: Yes. Some of my sisters are in Zambia. They went there with their husbands when this country was part of the Federation.

Morgan: The Federation of Rhodesia and Nyasaland?

Mutumwa: Yes.

Morgan: So you have relatives in Zambia?

Mutumwa: Many of them. They did not come back home at independence. Your father has not told you about them?

Morgan: No! Dad has not said anything about relatives in Zambia.

Mutumwa: Some of his sister's sons went to Tanzania in 1969 to join the liberation struggle.

Morgan: 1969?

Mutumwa: Yes. Unfortunately, the two boys died fighting somewhere in the north-eastern part of the country.

Morgan: *(excited).* Sekuru! We have relatives who died fighting to liberate this country?

Mutumwa: Yes. We have not been able to find out where they were buried and what Chimurenga names they used.

Morgan: No one has their names?

Mutumwa: They were called Farai and Jonasi Mukova.

Morgan: *(demandingly).* But somebody must know where Farai and Jonasi died fighting to liberate this land!

Mutumwa: It is not possible to know where they were buried. It no longer matters where they were buried. We know that they lie buried in the soil of the land they fought to liberate. What is important is for you all to know that your family has heroes of the liberation struggle whom we must always remember and honour.

Morgan: Thank you, Sekuru, for telling me all this. Thank you for telling me the story about my name. My name is a family history book. I will explain the meaning of Dzingai to my pastor. I am sure he will allow me to use both names: Morgan and Dzingai.

Mutumwa: It is good to hear you say that Shumba. It is you who must make the decision. Tell your pastor, the church, your parents and friends how they should call you. Tell them. "I am Dzingai! Dzingai Morgan Matanga."

Morgan: I will do that, Sekuru. Thank you for this knowledge about me and my family.

Mutumwa: That is good to hear Shumba. Remember you will also have to give the name Dzingai to your first son.

Morgan: What if I have no son, but just daughters?

Mutumwa: *(laughs).* You will have sons, Muzukuru! Even if it means marrying five wives just to have a son!

Morgan: (*laughs*). Five wives?

Mutumwa: Yes, Muzukuru. If your first wife does not give you a son, you get a second wife.

Morgan: *(laughing).* If the second wife does not give me a son, I get a third wife?

Mutumwa: *(laughs).* Because a son will carry our name Matanga to the future. You are the only son of my only son. Without a son, our name will be buried with you.

Morgan: That makes sense, Sekuru. It means I have no alternative but to marry and have a son.

Mutumwa: Yes. But not now, even though you can marry and have children.

Morgan: *(laughing).* Sekuru, I am only fourteen.

Mutumwa: *(laughing).* Shumba, take me to your room. I need to change these clothes, take a cold bath, sleep a little and wake up at six o'clock for my lovely cup of tea with bread, butter and jam.

Morgan: *(stands up).* This way, Sekuru.

Mutumwa: *(stands up).* By the way, Muzukuru, what is the meaning of Morgan?

Morgan: *(comes back to his grandfather laughing).* Come to think of it, I do not know what Morgan means.

Mutumwa: *(laughing).* So, how do you know that Morgan is a good name?

Morgan: I think dad and mum know the meaning of Morgan.

Mutumwa: You are telling me that your parents have not been comfortable with the idea of telling you the meaning of your name? Who can blame them? Eh? Your name could mean something frightening.

Morgan: Our pastor would not allow me to keep a frightening name. Morgan is a Christian name.

Mutumwa: *(laughs and grabs his grandson's hand).* Have you not heard Christian people with names such as Goliath, Jezebel, Nicodemus or Sodom?

Morgan: Christians named Goliath, Jezebel, Nicodemus and Sodom? *(Laughs.)* No Sekuru! No! Not in Zimbabwe! *(He begins to walk out.)*

Mutumwa: *(shouts laughing).* Come back Shumba! (*Morgan turns back.*) Sit down. I have something very important to ask you, Muzukuru!

(Morgan sits down on the same spot. He looks worried. Mutumwa speaks slowly and emphatically as he sits down.)

Mutumwa: Now, tell me. Is that your sister I saw standing about a hundred yards away from the gate to this house talking to a boy?

Morgan: Yes, *Sekuru*. That is Dorcas.

Mutumwa: Dorcas?

Morgan: Sorry. I mean Mufaro.

Mutumwa: And who is the boy?

Morgan: He is called Bernard.

Mutumwa: Who is he to your sister and to you?

Morgan: Well, eh...eh...he eh ...eh. He is ehh...eh....

Mutumwa: He is your sister's boyfriend. Isn't he?

Morgan: Yes. *(Pleading and almost whispering and showing fear.)* But, please, Sekuru, do not tell her that I am the one who told you that Bernard is her boyfriend!

Mutumwa: *(like a policeman, firmly and quickly).* Do your parents know about that?

Morgan: No. They do not know.

Mutumwa: What about your father's sister? Does she know?

Morgan: No. *Tete* Tendai does not know.

Mutumwa: What about your mother's younger sister? Does she know?

Morgan: Auntie Anastazia does not know.

Mutumwa: How did you know that Bernard is your sister's boyfriend?

Morgan: Bernard comes here very often when dad and mum are not here. He sits there where you are seated. She sits there too. They spend many hours together, talking and laughing. Sometimes holding hands and....

Mutumwa: *(angrily).* And you have been allowing him to come here and do that? *(Morgan is surprised.)* Eh? Has he married your sister?

Morgan: No.

Mutumwa: What is his surname?

Morgan: I do not know his surname. I only know that he is called Bernard.

Mutumwa: What is his totem?

Morgan: I don't know.

Mutumwa: What? You do not know his surname! You do not know his totem! What is wrong with you? Fine! Now, tell me! Where does he come from?

Morgan: He comes from Mount Pleasant.

Mutumwa: Mount Pleasant village under which chief?

Morgan: No, Sekuru. Mount Pleasant here in Harare.

Mutumwa: *(laughs).* Headman – Mount Pleasant! Chief – Mount Pleasant! District – Mount Pleasant! *(Furious and confronting Morgan.)* You do not know his totem? You do not know his surname! You do not know where he comes from? He is a total stranger to you? *(Harshly and very challenging.)* But you are the brother, Shumba! Why do you allow your sister to bring to your home a stranger whose surname and totem you do not know?

Morgan: She is my sister. Bernard is her friend, a boyfriend. How can I tell her not to eh… eh… eh?

Mutumwa: *(forcefully).* Shumba, when your father is not here, you are the man of house! You are your father! Your sister cannot bring anybody here whom she cannot bring when your father is here!

Morgan: It is difficult to tell my sister to stop eh... eh... eh.

Mutumwa: It cannot be difficult. Do you know why your sister only brings her boyfriend here when your mother and father are not here?

Morgan: I do not know why!

Mutumwa: *(shocked).* You do not know? Dzingai, you are fourteen! You are now a man.

Morgan: No, Sekuru. I am still called a child.

Mutumwa: *(harshly and confrontational).* Dzingai, are you a child? Eh? You are now a man! It seems that you do not know your place in this family. A few minutes ago, I said that you were not welcoming me properly to your home. I did not say your father's home. I said your home! A few years from now, you and your father will decide on the amount of *roora* to be paid for your sister. You will be expected to charge that stranger without a totem a lot of money for coming here and sitting on your sofas without your permission. Does that boy come here when you are not here?

Morgan: Yes, he does.

Mutumwa: Shumba! Don't you know that your sister and that that boy could do something bad here in this house? If that happens, will you tell the rest of the family that you allowed some stranger to come into your house and behave as if he had married your sister? *(Morgan shakes his head. Mutumwa holds his shoulder.)* Dzingai, this is your home! You are the only son. That sister of yours will be married and will leave you here. Do you understand that?

Morgan: *(emotionally).* Yes, Sekuru. I understand what you mean. But it is quite difficult to remember all these things you are saying and the role you expect me to play. It is all very complicated.

Mutumwa: *(emotionally).* Nothing is complicated! Just play your role, Shumba! *(Morgan stands up.)* Be a man! A responsible man of the house! *(Patting him on the back.)* I am here for three weeks and through that time I shall be watching you. Is that clear Shumba?

Morgan: Yes. It is clear, Sekuru!

Mutumwa: *(forcefully and frighteningly).* Be a man! Speak like a man, Dzingai. You are in your own house! You are a lion! Shumba! In your own den. ..the lion's den! You must roar. Is that clear, Dzingai? Roar!

Morgan: *(firmly and forcefully).* Yes. It is clear, Sekuru. *(Firmly and proudly.)* I am a lion! I am Shumba! And this is my den!

Mutumwa: *(claps hands, whistles and shouts). Hekani waro, Shumba! Mwana wechikara. Chokanyaira choenda Magare! Kumuka ndodzvova! Kutsika zvovava! Hekani waro* Charumbira![8] We hear your frightening roar! King of the Forest! You have spoken! *(Puts his hand around his shoulder and pulls him closer.)* Now Shumba, take me to your bedroom. I must sleep a little. *(Morgan leads his grandfather. He walks firmly and boldly. His grandfather pats him on the back with delight. They exit.)*

---

8. Behold the honoured one. Lion, the child of a beast. Walks proudly to its place at Magare! Waking up with a roar! Walking softly as if the ground is hot! Behold Charumbira, the praised one!

PART TWO

(Set in the same living room. Morgan enters. He is dressed in a tracksuit. He slumps into a sofa showing exhaustion. He sits back and relaxes. He is soon asleep. Dorcas and Bernard enter. Dorcas is dressed in a fancy pair of jean shorts and a school tracksuit jacket and sandals. Bernard is dressed in a jeans suit, fancy trainers and a baseball cap.)

Dorcas: *(speaks romantically and with gestures to signify welcome).* Please, sit down, Bernard.

Bernard: Just for five minutes.

Dorcas: Ok! Five minutes *(She hugs Bernard as a sign of being grateful.)*

Bernard: *(points at Morgan. Dorcas signals that he should not mind him. Bernard shakes his head. He signals that she should wake him up. He whispers).* Please, wake him up. I feel very uncomfortable with him here.

Dorcas: Please, feel at home. This is just Morgan. He is fast asleep!

Bernard: *(sitting down).* No! No! Please wake him up!

Dorcas: *(sitting down close to Bernard and puts her arm on his shoulder and getting closer to him).* Okay, I will wake him up after five minutes.

Bernard: No! Please Dorcas. Wake your brother up now. Please!

Dorcas: Okay. *(She goes to Morgan and shakes him up rather roughly.)* Wake up, Morgan! *(Morgan wakes up.)* Please, go to your bedroom!

Morgan: *(sees Bernard then suddenly stands up and confronts him aggressively).* Bernard?

Bernard: Yes, Morgan. Good afternoon.

Morgan: *(with force).* Bernard. Stand up and leave my house!

Dorcas: *(shocked).* What? Your house? What on earth are you talking about, Morgan?

Morgan: *(more forcefully and confrontationally).* Bernard. I said stand up and leave my house!

(Bernard stands up. Maidei enters and stands at a distance.)

Dorcas: *(forcefully).* Morgan, what are you doing?

Morgan: *(authoritatively).* I am sending Bernard away! He should not be here! He should leave my house!

(Dorcas confronts Bernard and speaks in a pleading voice.)

Dorcas: Don't listen to him, Bernard! Listen to me! Please, sit down.

(Bernard sits down. Morgan confronts Bernard.)

Morgan: Bernard! You are not wanted here! Don't you understand what I am saying? Are you deaf?

Bernard: *(stands up).* I understand what you are saying. I hear you very well, Morgan. You do not want to see me here! But what have I done wrong, Morgan? You have always welcomed me here. Have I done something I should not have done?

Morgan: *(instructively).* You are not supposed to be here! That is what is wrong!

Dorcas: *(confronting with fury).* Morgan, you have no right to say what you are saying and doing!

Maidei: *(confronting Dorcas).* No, Dorcas! You are wrong! Morgan has all the right to say what he has said and done! Morgan is...

Dorcas: *(disrespectful and confrontational).* And who gives you the right to get involved in this talk? Who the hell are you? Eh? You are a maid. Maidei, a house girl who should be in the kitchen right now! So get out of here!

Maidei: Sorry for saying this. Your brother is right. *(Turns to Bernard.)* Please Bernard, understand. Morgan is right to. . .

Dorcas: *(angrily).* Shut up, Maidei!

Bernard: *(trying to cool things down).* Okay, I am going out.

Dorcas: *(turns sharply to Bernard and shouts).* Bernard! You do not have to go, for goodness sake! This is my house and home also! I have a right to bring you here! You are my. . .

Bernard: I am sorry for causing trouble!

Dorcas: Bernard, you have not done anything wrong. You are not the cause of this trouble!

Bernard: I am sorry, I have to leave!

Dorcas: *(holding his hand).* No, Bernard. Don't leave! Please . . . *(Bernard pulls her towards the door. Dorcas pulls him back and shouts at Morgan.)* Morgan has no right to do what he is doing! (*Pleads with Bernard.*) Please, Bernard! Please, do not leave! Morgan cannot. . . . *(Bernard and Dorcas exit. Morgan stares blankly and in disbelief of what he has just done.)*

Maidei: *(ululates and dances a "mhembero"[9] dance shouting). Maita* Shumba! *Maita* Sipambi. *Maita mwana weChikara. Maita Charumbira!* (*She applauds him.*) You have done something today which you should have done a long time ago!

Morgan: *(shouting almost in tears).* That is my sister! My elder sister! I have been rude to her! I have shown disrespect to her in the presence of her boyfriend! I do not know how I am going to face her!

Maidei: *(laughs).* No, Shumba. You have done what is expected of you. I have always hoped you would do what you have just done. What you have done is to protect your sister and me!

Morgan: Protecting you from what?

---

9. Celebration dance with movements that express happiness.

Maidei: Morgan, if your parents had found out that your sister has been bringing boyfriends here for some time and that I had never told them, I would have been fired. From now on, Bernard is not going to come here. Your sister will never bring a boyfriend here. My job is safe and your sister is safe.

Morgan: *(desperately)*. But I am not safe from my sister's anger! She is going to kill me!

Maidei: Yes. She is going to come back burning with anger. She is going to fight you. So get ready to apologise as soon as she enters! Please do not challenge her! Do not say anything that will make her fight you. If she goes on to challenge you, tell her you are very sorry about what you have said and done. Show her the usual respect and if she wants to fight you, run out of the house and come back at 6.30 when your parents are back from work *(Clapping hands respectfully.)* Thank you, Shumba. Thank you, Sipambi! You are now a man of the house! *(She ululates and walks out to the kitchen. Morgan remains staring at her and then covers his face and slumps into the sofa, shaking his head. Dorcas enters walking hurriedly. She takes off her tracksuit jacket, folds it and throws it forcefully on Morgan's face.)*

Dorcas: What the hell was all that about, Morgan?

Morgan: *(pleading)*. Sisi Dorcas. I am very sorry about what I have said and done!

Dorcas: *(kicks him in the legs).* You are sorry? No! No! You are
            not sorry. Stand up and face me!

*(Morgan stands up and faces his sister holding his hands
together.)*

Morgan: Sisi Dorcas, I was wrong. Terribly wrong and....

Dorcas: *(she grabs the collar of his shirt and shouts into his
            face).* This is not your house, Morgan! I am the eldest
            child here! Do you understand what I am saying? I
            am your elder sister!

Morgan: Yes, I understand. I am very sorry about what I have
            said and done. I will. . . .

Dorcas: *(furious).* No! You are not sorry. I want you to tell me
            the truth, nothing but the whole truth! Why did you
            say and do what you did?

Morgan: *(pleading).* Please, cool down. You are too angry to
            hear anything I am going to say.

Dorcas: *(angrily and speaking into his face).* Angry? I am
            going to show you how angry I can become! You have
            never seen me that angry. Nobody has ever seen me
            that angry. *(She shakes her brother violently.)* Why
            did you chase Bernard away?

Morgan: Sisi Dorcas, I am terribly sorry.

Dorcas: You are not sorry. You cannot fool me. You are going
            to tell me the truth. . . nothing but the truth!

Morgan: *(gathers courage and shouts authoritatively).* Okay. Let me tell you the truth. You know my name? Dzingai. It means chase away! I have chased Bernard away!

Dorcas: *(laughs in disbelief. Leaves Morgan and abruptly turns away, then suddenly turns back and speaks angrily into his face).* Morgan, I am not joking! What happened is not a joke! *(Then suddenly steps back from Morgan.)* Oh, I see! You have gone crazy! You are possessed by some ancestral demon of Dzingai! *(She grabs him and shakes him.)* You are not Dzingai! You are Morgan! Morgan! Morgan!

Morgan: *(shouting firmly).* What is the surname of Bernard?

Dorcas: *(releases her grip on him but speaks into his face).* Why do you want to know that?

Morgan: *(shouting commandingly).* What is his surname?

Dorcas: *(shouting back with equal force).* I do not need to tell you anything about Bernard.

Morgan: If you do not tell me his surname, I will not tell you why I did what I did.

Dorcas: Morgan, you think this is some sort of a game, eh?

Morgan: My name is Dzingai Matanga! What is Bernard's surname?

Dorcas: *(relaxing but remaining very close to him and speaks with authority).* Okay! Bernard's surname is Shumba.

He is called Bernard Shumba. Now you know? Why did you. . . .

Morgan: *(forcefully).* What is his totem?

Dorcas: *(pushes Morgan down with force. Morgan falls onto the sofa. She follows him and shouts with anger).* What the hell are you talking about? What has Bernard got to do with totems? *(She grabs him to her feet by the collar of his shirt and shouts into his face.)* What is this rubbish about totems and Bernard?

Morgan: (*with urgency*). His totem could be lion, Shumba, just like you and me. He could be your brother.

Dorcas: My brother? Morgan, you have gone crazy! You are my brother, my only brother! *(She throws him down and shouts at him and uses her forefinger to poke his forehead furiously.)* Totems mean nothing to me! They mean nothing to Bernard! You cannot hide behind this issue of totems. You will tell me why you did what you did. I am going to make you tell me why you did what you did. *(Mutumwa enters. He is dressed in African shirt and khaki pair of trousers. He coughs to draw attention. Morgan points to him. Dorcas turns around and sees her grandfather walking towards them. She smiles.)*

Mutumwa: (*happily*). Mufaro, Muzukuru. You are around?

Dorcas: *(changing the tone to happiness).* Yes, Grandfather, I am around! *(Happily and going to him for a handshake.)* Welcome, Grandfather!

Mutumwa: *(he holds her hand and speaks happily).* Look at you, Muzukuru! You want to be taller than me. *(Morgan looks at them confused.)*

Dorcas: *(laughing happily).* I am going to be taller than you, Grandfather, I am still growing!

Mutumwa: MaSibanda, you are going to be as tall as my sister, Tambudzai, who was killed by an elephant in Gokwe in 1959. *(Laughs.)* And you look just like her. Everything, pretty face and a strong body!

Dorcas: *(laughs then holds his hand, and confronts him).* Grandfather, you called me MaSibanda?

Mutumwa: Yes, Shumba! Shumba women are called MaSibanda. *(Taking Dorcas to a seat.)* Your uncle James Gumbo is a Madyirapazhe. Your mother is MaGumbo. *(They both sit down.)*

Dorcas: But you have never called me MaSibanda before?

Mutumwa: *(laughs).* There shall always be a first time. First day for something for you as you grow up. It is time we call you MaSibanda, Muzukuru.

Morgan: Grandfather, are you saying Madyirapazhe and MaGumbo are the same.

Mutumwa: *(happily).* Yes, Muzukuru, just as Shumba and MaSibanda are the same.

Dorcas: How are you, Grandfather?

Mutumwa: MaSibanda, stand up. Come here and kneel down and shake my hand in a proper greeting.

Dorcas: *(stands up and goes to a spot in front of her grandfather. She kneels down and extends a hand for a handshake. Mutumwa grabs the hand).* Greetings, grandfather!

Mutumwa: *(shouting and shaking her hand enthusiastically). Mhoro,* Muzukuru!

Dorcas: How are you, Sekuru?

Mutumwa: Clap your hands, Muzukuru!

Dorcas: *(clapping her hands like a man).* How are you, Sekuru?

Mutumwa: *(laughs).* You are clapping like a man!

Dorcas: Oh, sorry. *(She claps her hands like a woman.)*

Mutumwa: *(happily).* I am well, MaSibanda. How are you, Muzukuru?

Dorcas: I am fine, Sekuru!

(Mutumwa signals that Dorcas can go back to her seat. Dorcas goes to her seat.)

Morgan: *(alert and smiling)*. Sekuru, can a Shumba man marry a Shumba woman - a MaSibanda?

Mutumwa: A Shumba man cannot marry a Shumba woman. They are brother and sister. That would be incest if they marry.

Dorcas: *(taking a defensive stance and challenging her grandfather)*. What if the Shumba man's parents come all the way from Mutoko, in the east, and the Shumba woman's parents come from Gutu, in the south? These are total strangers. They are Shumba but are not related. Why can they not be allowed to marry?

Mutumwa: *(laughs)*. Oh MaSibanda. . . you make me laugh. *(Lecturing.)* Have they not taught you at school about totems and what they mean? The Shumba people in Gutu, Charumbira, Chirumanzu, Mutoko, Chivi, Domboshava and Mutasa are the same Lion people. They may be Shumba Nyamuziwa, Shumba Sipambi, Shumba Mhazi or Shumba Murambwi. They are all one family. They cannot marry. That would be incest. *(Maidei enters with a teapot, tea cups, slices of bread and jam on a tray. Mutumwa signals her to stop before she gets to the coffee table.)* Thank you, Muzukuru, for making my tea. My wife is here. You should not bother serving me the tea yourself, Soko.

Maidei: *(laughing joyfully)*. Sorry, Shumba. I totally forgot.

Dorcas: *(excitedly).* Grandmother is here? *(Maidei and Mutumwa laugh. Dorcas and Morgan are surprised. They stare at their grandfather and Maidei, laughing.)*

Maidei: You are the wife, Dorcas!

Dorcas: Me?

Mutumwa: Yes, you are my wife!

Dorcas: I am your granddaughter, Sekuru!

(Mutumwa and Maidei laugh. Dorcas and Morgan are surprised. Maidei walks out to the kitchen with the tray, laughing. Mutumwa gets back to lecturing to his grandchildren.)

Mutumwa: If the Shumba man and the Shumba woman who want to marry know that they are both Shumba, their parents conduct a ceremony to cut the relationship. It is called *chekaukama* - cutting of the relationship. At the ceremony, they slaughter a completely white cow that has not given birth. The white cow must be provided by the man. The marrying couple drinks the raw blood of the white cow to remove the relationship from each other and to make them strangers.

Morgan: They drink raw blood?

Mutumwa:Yes, the ritual of *chekaukama* is complicated. Sometimes finding a white cow from our traditional cattle is not easy.

Morgan: You mean the cow has to be of indigenous stock - the MaShona stock?

Mutumwa:Yes! One hundred percent indigenous! It is slaughtered, roasted and eaten without adding salt to it.

(Morgan and Dorcas laugh. Maidei enters and she claps hands in respect to Mutumwa.)

Maidei: *Pamusoroi* Shumba. Sorry for intruding. May I speak to Dorcas?

Mutumwa: Go ahead, Muzukuru. Speak to her.

(Maidei goes to Dorcas and whispers into her ears that she should go to the kitchen to bring the tea to her grandfather. Dorcas is shocked and abruptly speaks to Maidei in an angry whisper.)

Dorcas: *(whispering harshly).* You want me to do what? That is your job, Sisi. I am not your assistant.

(Maidei and Mutumwa begin to laugh. Morgan and Dorcas are surprised. Maidei sits down. Mutumwa turns to Morgan and begins to lecture to him. Dorcas and Maidei turn to Mutumwa's address.)

Mutumwa: *(holding Morgan's hand).* Shumba, what is happening here? It seems your sister did not realise that when I said my wife was here, I meant her, Mufaro Matanga. When I am here, your sister should handle me like her future husband. She should cook what I eat. She should serve all the food that I eat. It is not the duty of

Maidei here or any other worker. There can be plenty of workers here who can do other things, but not serving me food or making me tea when your sister is here. All my granddaughters are my wives in that sense. I do not marry them. Not in that sense of husband. They just have to treat me the way they will treat their husbands.

Dorcas: *(pleading).* I am sorry, Sekuru. I am sorry for the ignorance. *(Turns to Maidei.)* I am sorry, Sisi! *(Maidei holds her hand and takes her to the kitchen.)*

Morgan: Sekuru, we have a lot to learn.

Mutumwa: We are all learning. Learning does not end. Older people like me have a lot more to learn than you, Muzukuru. We have to learn all this technology that is changing every day. We cannot catch up with …cellphone, iPad, laptop, broad band, Wi-Fi, this model, and that model *(Morgan laughs. Mutumwa laughs along.)*

Morgan: Sekuru, let us make a deal.

Mutumwa: What deal?

Morgan: You teach me everything I need to know, – our people, our way of doing things. I will teach you all that I know about computers and the Internet.

Mutumwa: I do not have a computer.

Morgan: We have a desktop which you can use.

Mutumwa: A desk?

Morgan: A desktop is a computer, there. Then, there is a laptop – a portable computer.

Mutumwa: Yes, I agree to the deal. You teach me computers and I teach you all you need to know!

(They shake their hands excitedly. Maidei and Dorcas enter. Dorcas is carrying a tray with tea. Maidei is carrying a dish of water and a towel. Dorcas puts the tray on the coffee table then goes to sit down. Maidei goes to sit near Dorcas.)

Mutumwa: It seems I have a lot to learn while I am here.

Morgan: I too have a lot to learn. I have already learnt a lot, Sekuru.

Mutumwa: I came here by taxi. I told the driver that I was going to Borrowdale. He said this place is known as Borrowdale West.

Morgan: *(animated).* Yes, Sekuru. I nearly corrected you earlier when you said that our home here is in Borrowdale. This is Borrowdale West.

Mutumwa: Another Borrow's village? Why? This is a new residential area built after independence. Why should this area be another Borrow's village? Dzingai, do you know who Borrow was?

Morgan: Borrow was a person?

Mutumwa: You do not know that?

Morgan: No, I never heard of that.

Morgan: You did not learn that in your history lessons?

Morgan: No.

Mutumwa: *(with anger)*. What type of history do they teach you at school? History about Europe and America?

Dorcas: I know about Borrow, Sekuru. He was part of the pioneer column. He was among the colonialists who fought the Ndebele in the war of the early 1890s.

Mutumwa. Yes, Muzukuru. That is the history. The story of the Anglo-Ndebele War. . . . The Battle of Bembesi . . . . The Battle of Pupu! Borrowdale means Borrow's valley.

Morgan: So Borrowdale West means the western valley of Borrow.

Mutumwa: *(harshly to Dorcas)*. Muzukuru, have you run out of names to use in naming residential areas in this city that you continue using Borrow's name?

Dorcas: *(defensively)*. It is not us who name residential areas, Sekuru. It is the City Council and, eh....

Mutumwa: *(challenging)*. What about the names of the streets in this suburb? What are they called?

Morgan: Zebra!

Dorcas: Kudu!

Morgan: Giraffe!

Maidei: Elephant!

Mutumwa: *(laughs).* What is wrong with you people? We have thousands of liberation heroes but you choose to name your streets Zebra, Rhino, Giraffe, Kudu and Elephant. At independence, you found roads like Selous, Salisbury and Prince Edward. Don't you know your heroes even those who fought Borrow, Bowden Powell, Courtney Selous and Allan Wilson?

Morgan: *(forcefully).* It is not us who name these streets.

Dorcas: We are never consulted.

Mutumwa: Why didn't you tell them that these streets should be named after the heroes who lie at National Heroes Acre and at provincial heroes acres all over this country? Why don't you tell the city council that you want the names of your streets changed?

Dorcas: But where can we tell them? *(Suddenly realising.)* Come to think of it, Grandfather, the government and the city council have run out of names even for schools built after independence. They have schools named Seke High 1. Seke High 2. Seke High 3.

Morgan: Dzivarasekwa 1, Dzivarasekwa 2.

Maidei: Glen Norah 6, Glen Norah 7.

Dorcas: Kuwadzana High I, Kuwadzana High 10.

Mutumwa: That is terrible. Why don't students who go to such secondary schools ask the government for proper names for their schools?

Morgan: *(getting excited).* You mean students can do that? Ask the government to change the names of their schools?

Mutumwa: *(excitedly).* Why not? How can students accept their school to be called Glen Norah High10?

Morgan: *(enthusiastically).* Instead of being called Nehanda Secondary School.

Mutumwa: Or Safiriyo Madzikatire Secondary School!

Dorcas: Safiriyo Madzikatire? A national hero?

Mutumwa: You do not know who Safiriyo Madzikatire was?

Dorcas: I am sorry, grandfather. A national hero called Madzikatire? I honestly do not know him.

(Maidei enters.)

Morgan: You have never heard of Safiriyo Madzikatire the musician – the legend?

Dorcas: He played *sungura* music, eh?

Morgan: I do not think so. *(Turns to Mutumwa.)* What music did Safiriyo Madzikatire play, *Sekuru*?

Mutumwa: Safiriyo Madzikatire played Zimbabwean music. He produced drama on radio and television. He was a dramatist and a comedian. He was called Mukadota.

Dorcas: Oh him! Oh, he was funny! Very funny! His television drama was in Shona.

Mutumwa: He was a great entertainer who was loved by all.

(*Maidei goes to Dorcas and whispers to her.*)

Dorcas: *(surprised).* Oh! I am sorry. *(She stands up. Maidei holds her hands and guides her to the coffee table.)*

Maidei: *(clapping hands).* Shumba, sorry for interrupting your talk with your grandchildren. This special tea with bread, butter and jam is yours.

Mutumwa: *(laughing).* Oh! That is for me?

Maidei: I am sorry that your wife forgot to tell you that this is your meal. I have just been waiting for her to do so.

Mutumwa: *(laughs).* Let her proceed to serve me then.

Maidei: Over to you, Dorcas.

Dorcas: *(laughing).* I do not know where to start. I do not want to continue making mistakes. Honestly, I need help.

Mutumwa: *(laughing).* People who fear to make mistakes never do anything special in life.

(Dorcas goes to open the plates. Maidei holds her hands and stops her.)

Maidei: Start by clapping your hands to honour the person who made the meal. I am a Soko Wachenuka. I made the meal. I am here. So you do this. *(Claps hands and shouts.) Pamusoroi Soko.*[10] Mukanya! *(Then proceeds to remove the embroidered cloth. She takes the dish of water and towel.) Pamusoroi* Shumba, please wash your hands for this meal of tea. *(Mutumwa washes his hands smiling and dries them.)* Now clap your hands and open the plates. *(Dorcas claps her hands and opens the plates.)*

Mutumwa: *(claps hands and speaks warmly).* Thank you, MaSibanda. *(Maidei stands up to leave. Dorcas stands up.)*

Maidei: Dorcas, you have not finished. *(Dorcas goes down to her knees. Maidei sits down on sofa.)* Pour the tea and milk into the cup and ask him how many teaspoons of sugar he takes. *(Dorcas pours the tea and milk into a cup, then looks.)*

Dorcas: How many teaspoons of sugar?

Maidei: Clap your hands and say, 'Shumba how many teaspoons of sugar should I put into your tea?'

Mutumwa: *(with a big smile).* Thank you, MaSibanda. Four teaspoons of sugar will do.

---

10.   Excuse me, Monkey.

(Dorcas puts four teaspoons of sugar and then puts the teaspoon in the saucer.)

Maidei: You have not finished, MaSibanda. Stir the tea.

Dorcas: Oh. *(She picks up the spoon and stirs the tea continuously.)*

Mutumwa: MaSibanda, that is enough stirring. *(Maidei laughs, Dorcas and Morgan join in laughing.)*

Dorcas: *(laughing).* Is there anything else I need to do?

Mutumwa: Do you want to join me in drinking tea?

Dorcas: Do I have to do that?

(Maidei and Mutumwa laugh.)

Mutumwa: Thank you, MaSibanda. You have served me adequately.

(Dorcas is happy with herself. She smiles happily and stands up. Morgan joins in smiling. Dorcas stands up. Maidei shows her respect and walks out. Dorcas sits down, then watches Mutumwa eat and drink. Dorcas and Morgan make gestures to each other to signal that their grandfather should not be disturbed. Dorcas clears her throat and speaks.)

Dorcas: Sekuru, I have some homework to do.

Mutumwa: You are free to leave me now. Go and do your homework.

(Tendai Matanga enters. She is dressed in a security guard uniform which shows that she is a senior member of the organisation. She rushes to Mutumwa shouting excitedly.)

Tendai: Baba, welcome!

Mutumwa: *(equally excited).* Thank you, my daughter!

(Tendai rushes to kneel before her father, holds the wrist of the right hand with the left hand and holds Mutumwa's right hand at the wrist for a handshake. They shake hands enthusiastically.)

Tendai: *Mhoroi*, Baba![11]

Mutumwa: *Mhoro*, Tendai *mwanangu!*[12] *(They finish the hand-shake. Tendai stands up and rushes to sit on the sofa closer to Dorcas.)*

Dorcas: Good evening, Tete!

Tendai: Good evening, Dorcas!

Morgan: Good evening, Tete!

Tendai: Good evening, Morgan. *(She turns to her father clapping her hands.)* How are you, father?

Mutumwa: I am very well, my daughter. How are you?

Tendai: I am well, Baba. How are they at home?

Mutumwa: They are all well. They were greeting you!

Tendai: Thank you. We are all fine.

---

11.   Greetings, father
12.   Greetings, Tendai, my child.

Morgan: *(speaks firmly).* Sekuru! We will talk later about the Dzingai story. I will use my cellphone to record the story.

Mutumwa: *(excitedly).* Yes, Dzingai. We shall talk. I will tell you more about Mukudzei Matanga, the father of my father, who died fighting the Germans in East Africa in the First World War.

Morgan: *(excitedly).* A Matanga fought the Germans?

Mutumwa: Yes, Mukudzei Matanga fought the Germans in the 1914-1918 War.

Morgan: Wow! We have a lot to talk about, Sekuru! First World War, 1914, Second World War, 1945. The Second Chimurenga.

Mutumwa: *(excitedly).* Yes, Shumba. We have a lot to talk about you and the Matanga family.

Tendai: Morgan, I did not know that you were interested in our history?

Morgan: *(firmly).* Yes, Tete. But, first, let me correct you. My name is Dzingai. Dzingai Morgan Matanga. You can also call me Shumba!

Mutumwa: *(clapping hands).* Well-spoken, Shumba! *(Tendai joins in clapping her hands and ululating. Morgan walks away in a firm, imposing and very manly manner.)*

Dorcas: *(stands up)*. Sekuru, I have some homework to do! See you later.

Mutumwa: Do your homework. We shall find time to talk.

Dorcas: That will be nice, Sekuru. I hope you have a special family story for me, especially about your sister who was killed by an elephant in Gokwe.

Mutumwa: *(laughing)*. There are many family stories for you.

Dorcas: I would love to hear them, Sekuru. I am interested in the stories of the women members of our family.

Tendai: Baba, your Muzukuru is a feminist.

Mutumwa: She is a what?

Tendai: A feminist. She believes in the empowering of women.

Mutumwa: What is that?

(Tendai and Dorcas laugh. They realise that Mutumwa is not joking.)

Tendai: Your Muzukuru will find time to explain what the idea of empowering women is all about.

Dorcas: Yes, Sekuru. I will explain.

Mutumwa: I hope it is not one of those strange foreign ideas about women's liberation. I mean, those ideas about women who do not want to be married by men.

(Tendai and Dorcas laugh.)

Tendai: It is not those ideas, *baba*.

Mutumwa: Alright. I will find time to listen to her explanation. Do not fear to frighten me with your ideas!

(Dorcas and Tendai laugh.)

Tendai: Shumba, I am afraid that you are not ready to hear about women empowerment which your Muzukuru will talk to you about.

Mutumwa: Empowerment means giving power to women. Why should I be afraid of that? All the *tetes* are empowered to make decisions.

Dorcas: You mean *tete* like *tete* here? She has powers?

Mutumwa: Yes, many powers.

Tendai: Dorcas, you will have to talk to your grandfather later. I need a few minutes with him now.

Dorcas.   Okay. Thanks Tete. See you later, Sekuru. *(She walks out.)*

Tendai: I came here two days ago. I am attending a course. I will leave tonight for Kuwadzana.

Mutumwa: Mai Farai, did you know that your brother's daughter brings a boyfriend here when the parents are away?

Tendai: Dorcas has a boyfriend?

Mutumwa: She brings the boyfriend here!

Tendai: She told you that?

Mutumwa: Telling me what?

Tendai: *(inquisitively).* How did you know about that, Baba?

Mutumwa: Does it matter who told me? This afternoon, I found her at the entrance to this house holding hands with her boyfriend.

Tendai: Dorcas was holding the hands of a boy here?

Mutumwa: You seem to know nothing about your brother's daughter. How come she has not told you about her boyfriend, somebody she brings here? The boy sits on that sofa, your brother's seat. They behave as if they are husband and wife.

Tendai: Baba, I do not stay here. I come here for one or two days.

Mutumwa: *(forcefully and challenging).* Your brother's daughter is 16 years old and you know nothing about her! How do you know that she is still alright? Have you examined her?

Tendai: Examine?

Mutumwa: Yes. Just as your *tete* Mai Dambudzo did to you. She took you to the river, examined you to make sure that you were still a virgin when you finished school.

Tendai: Baba. I am very sorry. I will not do that!

Mutumwa: *(getting angry).* What did you say?

Tendai: I will not take Dorcas to a river or a lake. I will not examine her!

Mutumwa: How will you know that she is still a virgin?

Tendai: Baba. Please, forgive me. What I am going to say may make you angry but I have to say it! I am not being disrespectful of you!

Mutumwa: I will not get angry, my daughter. I will listen to every word you will say.

Tendai: Baba, you already sound and look angry.

Mutumwa: I am sorry, MaSibanda. I am not angry. I am just concerned. I mean, anxious.

Tendai: Okay, you are concerned. Baba, times are changing. Times have changed. I did not protest to you or my mother about what Tete Mai Dambudzo did to me to establish that I was still a virgin. That is because I grew up respecting all your decisions and all that you said were our ways of doing things - our culture. I was very disappointed and hurt that you, my mother, and your sisters did not believe me when I said that I was still a virgin. You did not trust that I could still be a virgin at 18 years of age.

Mutumwa: What are you saying, my daughter? My sister examined you and found that you were still a virgin before we began talking about your marriage to Zindoga. We were all very happy. We congratulated your *tete* Mai Dambudzo. She was very happy with you! Are you now telling me that my sister was wrong to declare you a virgin at that time?

Tendai: *(trying hard to suppress her emotional build up).* Father, why did you not trust me? Why did you think that all that I said about myself was a lie? I had looked after myself, not for you, my mother, your sisters or future husband. I had taken care of myself because . . . .

Mutumwa: *(shouts angrily).* Wait a minute, Tendai! You are talking to me. Your father!

Tendai: That is why I asked for your forgiveness.

Mutumwa: *(angrily).* You are talking to me!

Tendai: Yes, I have to say this. I wish I was talking to Tete Mai Dambudzo!

Mutumwa: Do you trust your brother's daughter?

Tendai: *(angrily).* Father, we are talking about me and not Dorcas.

Mutumwa: *(angrily).* We are not talking about you, Tendai. We are talking about your brother's daughter. . . your responsibility . . . .The one who is bringing a boyfriend here and spending many hours in each other's arms on these sofas!

Tendai: Father, you cannot continue to think that our way of doing things cannot change, should not change and is not changing. You have to accept that there are things we did at home in Gutu, thirty years ago, which we cannot do anymore. I have not inspected Dorcas to see if she is still a virgin or not. I will not do that! But I have sat down with her and talked to her about looking after herself and about protection.

Mutumwa: Protection? You are telling her about protection?

Tendai: Father, you did not trust me when I was 17 years old but I trusted you and believed everything you said. I ask you now to trust me with my responsibility for Dorcas. I know what is expected of me. Leave me to play my role as *tete* here in Harare and in the present circumstances. I know and respect our traditions . . . our ways of doing things but there are many things we cannot continue to hold on to because they are changing with time, even if we want to keep them as they were during your boyhood days and my girlhood times. *(Mutumwa stares at his daughter, nodding.)* I thank you for reminding me about my responsibility as a *tete*. Baba, I am attending a company reception. After the function, I will go to Kuwadzana. I will come back to see you on Saturday morning, Shumba.

Mutumwa: But we have not finished discussing. I want to be assured that you are playing your role adequately as *tete* to these children.

Tendai: *(agitated)*. Honestly, Baba, how do I play my role when the children are not allowed to visit me in Kuwadzana Township?

Mutumwa: *(shocked)*. What? Your brother's children are not allowed to visit their *tete*?

Tendai: The children are not allowed to visit me or Mai Chiedza[13] in Mutare.

Mutumwa: Who stops them from visiting you? Your brother or his wife?

Tendai: My brother has no say in such matters. It is his wife who makes all the decisions. That woman has cooked him, Baba! Your son cannot even raise a finger at her! He is just like one of the children, I tell you! Baba, you should find time to talk to him. Poor relatives are relatives. My husband is not rich. He does not earn much as a policeman but my brother should respect him as a *mukuwasha*[14] who should be visited even if he lives in a one-bedroom house. If we did not come here, nobody would know that Joseph Matanga is my brother. Baba, if you cannot do anything to help my brother, please ask Sekuru Zinyemba to come here and have a word with him or do something to make him head of the family again.

13.   Mother of Chiedza
14.   Son-in-law

Mutumwa: *(angrily).* What is wrong with you, Tendai? You are *tete!* Your brother's wife is your wife. You are the husband. You do not ask her for the children to come to your home. You do not ask your brother. You tell your wife that you want the children with you!

Tendai: Baba! It is not that simple.

Mutumwa: *(with anger).* The problem with you is that you do not understand or appreciate your responsibilities as *tete.*

Tendai: Baba, these are not my children.

Mutumwa: What are you talking about? Are they your wife's children? They are Gumbo Madyirapazhe?[15]

Tendai: No. They are Shumba.

Mutumwa: So what are you talking about?

Tendai: But these children . . . .

Mutumwa: *(angrily).* There is no but . . . .Know your responsibilities as *tete!* Do not give me excuses. When your husband's sister visits your family, what does she do?

Tendai: Tete Mai Chenjerai[16] is rough with me and rough with my children.

Mutumwa: She is not rough. She is your husband and makes the children know who she is.

Tendai: But, Baba, she is....

---

15.   The leg people who ate their meals outside while looking out for the invaders.
16.   Auntie, the mother of Chenjerai.

Mutumwa: *(angrily).* No, but Tendai! Do not make me angry!

Tendai: I am sorry, Baba. I am sorry. I understand what you are saying. I will take my place as *tete* of these children. *(She turns to face the bedrooms and shouts.)* Dorcas! Morgan! *(She pauses, then shouts again.)* Dorcas! *(Maidei enters carrying a dish.)* Sisi Maidei, tell my brother that I will come back on Saturday morning!

Maidei: *(kneeling down in front of the coffee table).* Tete, are you going without eating anything? I am preparing . . . .

Tendai: I am going to a company reception. There will be plenty to eat there. *(Turns to her father with a smile.)* See you on Saturday, Shumba. Have a pleasant stay here, Baba.

Mutumwa: Thank you, my daughter, for coming. I have heard you! I have learnt a lot from what you have said. Learning does not end. *(Maidei puts the cups into the dish slowly but inquisitively following the discussion.)*

Tendai: *(laughing).* Learning, Baba? There is nothing to learn from what I said. *(She goes down on her knees and speaks emotionally.)* Baba. Thank you for allowing me to say what I said to you this evening. I never thought that you would allow me to say such things to you directly. I know that if mother was here, she would have been very angry with me. She would have shouted at me to get out of here!

Mutumwa: *(laughing).* Mai Farai. You are *tete,* not only to these children, but to your brothers and to me your father as well.

Tendai: *(excitedly).* Tete to you? Is that so, *baba*?

Mutumwa: Yes, my daughter. You are *tete* to all of us. In the presence of the children, I do not call you Mai Farai or Tendai but tete!

(Loud horn of a car is sounded and Tendai reacts sharply.)

Tendai: *(excitedly).* That's my taxi, *baba! (She claps hands to take her leave.)* Thank you, Shumba! See you on Saturday. Stay well, Baba.

Mutumwa: Travel well, MaSibanda. Bring me my grandchildren on Saturday!

Tendai: *(standing up).* I will do that, *baba.* They will be delighted to see you. Goodbye!

(She picks up her handbag and walks out hurriedly.)

Maidei: *(holding a dish and speaking with emotion).* Sekuru, I wish I had a father like you! *(Mutumwa laughs.)* I heard you and Tete Mai Farai talk. You allowed her to speak out her mind, Sekuru. That was good, Sekuru. Mai Farai spoke for many of us.

Mutumwa: So you heard everything we said, Muzukuru?

Maidei: I was lucky, Sekuru, to hear everything you said while not here.

Mutumwa: I want to stretch my legs in the garden, Muzukuru. I am glad that you found it useful - what my daughter and I said to each other. *(He stands up.)* In Shona, they say a servant also learns from hearing the master instructing his son!

Maidei: It was as if you were talking to me, Shumba! *(Emotionally.)* I have my brother's daughters who are educated. They do not think that they should listen to me. Whenever I try to tell them what not to do they laugh at me.

Mutumwa: I am sorry to hear that, Muzukuru. *(Firmly and stooping to look into her eyes.)* You are their *tete*, Muzukuru. No one is going to take your place of being *tete*. Do you understand what I am saying? You are *tete* to these children of your boss.

Maidei: Is that so, Sekuru?

Mutumwa: Yes, you look after these children. You should be a *tete* to them. Advise them. Correct them. Their parents are not here all the time.

Maidei: Yes, Sekuru. I understand what you mean.

Mutumwa: Play your role as *tete* without fear. Talk to them in Shona. Talk to them anytime you are with them! Never give up! Never get tired of playing your role as *tete*! If your brother's daughters become terrible wives and mothers in future, you will bear the blame for that.

Maidei: I know that, Sekuru.

Mutumwa: Therefore, do not allow anyone to prevent you from doing your job of making your brothers' daughters know what it is to become women.

Maidei: Thank you, Sekuru. I will not allow anyone to do that.

Mutumwa: Remember, you are also *tete* to these children here. When you are here as the only adult, these children should see you as their *tete*.

Maidei: To these children, I am just their maid, Sekuru!

Mutumwa: You should not make yourself a maid but their *tete*. Do you understand what I am saying?

Maidei: How do I do that?

Mutumwa: *(instructively).* Just be a *tete* to them! Advise them! Instruct them. Correct them! Be their guide! When you see them doing wrong things, tell them the right things right away. You are not only *tete* to your brothers' children. Bringing up a child is the responsibility of the whole village. You are the village to these children. Do you understand what I am saying, Muzukuru?

Maidei: I understand what you mean, Sekuru. You are wise,
            Sekuru. I respect your wisdom. I will do what you have
            said.

Mutumwa: Good to hear you say that, Muzukuru. When the
            chief is advising or teaching his children, any servants
            that are present also learn from the chief's wisdom.

Maidei: *(excitedly)*. You are right, Sekuru. . . you are wise.

Mutumwa: *(he calls)*. Dzingai!

Maidei: Sekuru, let me go and call him.

Mutumwa: You mean he cannot hear me in this house? *(Shouts
            louder.)* Dzingai!

Maidei: He hears you, Sekuru.

Mutumwa: Why do you want to go and call him when he can
            hear me?

(Maidei laughs. Mutumwa laughs with her.)

Morgan: *(enters, shouting)*. Yes!

Mutumwa: What did you say?

Morgan: Did you call me?

Mutumwa: What did you say to my call?

Morgan: I said, yes.

Mutumwa: Yes, what?

Morgan: Yes, Sekuru!

Mutumwa: *(showing annoyance)*. You do not say 'yes' to me! You shout back saying "I am coming, Sekuru!" Say that!

Morgan: *(he shouts)*. I am coming, Sekuru!

Mutumwa: Good. Now that you are here, take me to your garden!

Morgan: Garden?

Mutumwa: Yes. Take me to your garden!

Morgan: Sekuru, I do not have a garden!

(Maidei laughs, stops and comes back still holding the tray with the cups. Morgan is surprised.)

Mutumwa: What did you say?

Morgan: I do not have a garden, Sekuru.

Mutumwa: Whose garden is that behind your house?

Morgan: Oh, you mean that. There is a gardener. Johannes is his name.

Mutumwa: What? That garden there belongs to Johannes?

Morgan: No. Johannes is employed as a gardener. He works in that garden.

Mutumwa: Do you work in that garden?

Morgan: No. I do not work in the garden.

Mutumwa: What? You do not work in the garden?

Morgan: No.

Mutumwa: Does your sister work in the garden?

Morgan: No.

Mutumwa: Does your mother work in the garden?

Morgan: No.

Mutumwa: Does your father work in the garden?

Morgan: No. Only Johannes works in the garden.

Mutumwa: *(laughs. Maidei joins the laughter).* You all eat what you do not grow?

Morgan: What do you mean, *Sekuru*?

Mutumwa: You eat what you do not grow?

Morgan: Everything in that garden is grown by Johannes.

Mutumwa: How old is Johannes?

Morgan: He must be about fifty to sixty years old. He is a grandfather.

Mutumwa: And you call him Johannes?

Morgan: I do not know his surname.

Maidei: He is called Johannes Mutero.

Mutumwa: You did not know that?

Morgan: No. I do not know that. Father calls him Johannes.

Maidei: No. Your mother calls him Johannes but your father calls him Madyirapazhe.

Mutumwa: *(surprised).* He is a Madyirapazhe?

Maidei: Yes, his totem is Gumbo.

Mutumwa: Dzingai! That gardener is your uncle. He is of your mother's totem, Gumbo! That gardener is your mother's brother. He is your uncle.

Morgan: *(shouting almost in anger).* Nobody told me that! How am I expected to know these things without being told? That man has been a gardener here for more than ten years.

Maidei: Sorry, I should have told you. It is my fault. I am sorry.

Mutumwa: *(holds Morgan's hand and pulls him closer to him and pats him on his back).* Shumba, do not get angry with your parents and me. Remember this. Children do not learn only at school. This house, this family, is a big teaching and learning school. More than three quarters of what you need to know about us, about yourself, our family and our extended family is taught here in this school. What you are going to teach your children is what you learn from right here. Is that clear?

Morgan: It makes a lot of sense, Sekuru. At school, we do not learn all these things you have been saying to me and my sister.

Mutumwa: Now take me to your garden. What is growing in the garden?

Morgan: I do not know.

Mutumwa: You do not know?

Morgan: I do not know anything growing in the garden.

Mutumwa: Why don't you know?

Morgan: Sekuru, the garden is not my business.

(Dorcas enters, working on her cellphone.)

Mutumwa. *(in anger).* Don't be stupid, Dzingai! Everything here is your business! The garden is part of your property. You have to know what your property is and what is going on in your property. You are the man of the house! *(He pushes him.)* Let's go. *(Morgan leads him out.)*

Dorcas: *(shouts to Maidei).* Morgan is the man of the house?

Maidei: Yes. He is the man of the house!

Dorcas: *(challenging).* And me? What am I? Woman of the what?

Maidei: *(laughing).* Woman of the kitchen!

Dorcas: *(protesting).* No! I have as much right to everything in this house as Morgan.

Maidei: Morgan is a man. You are a woman. You will be married. You will leave this place to your brother. You will leave the name Matanga here and take the name of your husband.

Dorcas: Who made that decision? *(Maidei laughs. Dorcas confronts her.)* Sisi, I am not joking! Who made that stupid decision?

Maidei: At the marriage ceremony, during the night of your wedding, your husband's parents will ask your parents to allow them to take you away from here to go and belong to their family. That is why they will have paid *roora.*

Dorcas: What if I refuse to have them pay *roora*[17] for me? *(Maidei laughs.)* What if I pay the *roora* myself and not my husband? *(Maidei laughs.)* What if I tell my parents that my husband and I will want to live here with them? *(Maidei laughs. Dorcas stares at her.)*

Maidei: You and your husband living here as what? Children?

Dorcas: When Morgan marries, will he live here with his wife?

Maidei: Yes, if he wants to.

---

17.   Bride price

Dorcas: Live here with our parents?

Maidei: Yes.

Dorcas: *(authoritatively).* If Morgan can be allowed to live here with our parents, our family, why should I not be allowed to live here with my family?

Maidei: You do not bring your husband here. You are not the one who marries a man. You are the one a man marries and takes away to his family, his people.

Dorcas: *(shouts).* That is so unfair!

Maidei: Unfair? *(She laughs.)*

Dorcas: A man does not marry a woman. A man and a woman get married!

Maidei: *(laughing).* Dorcas! You are going to be married by a man. You do not marry a man. You get married by a man.

Dorcas: That is the language that must change.

Maidei: It is not the language we are talking about. We are talking about our traditions – our way of doing things.

Dorcas: We will change these traditions that do not make sense. *(Maidei laughs.)* I shall lead the young women of this country in a revolution to change the meaningless customs and traditions, especially those that make women inferior to men.

Maidei: *(laughing).* You want to start another Chimurenga?

Dorcas: Yes. It will be called Mbuya Nehanda Women Empowerment Revolution!

Mutumwa: *(maidei laughs. Mutumwa and Morgan enter. Mutumwa is furious and shouts).* Dzingai, you are no longer a child! You are now a man! *(He waves a bunch of green leaves to him.)* What type of vegetable is this?

Morgan: To tell you the truth, Sekuru, I do not know what that plant is!

Mutumwa: *(he hands over the bunch of leaves to Morgan).* What you are holding Muzukuru Dzingai,[18] is *mbanje.*[19]

Morgan: What?

Mutumwa: Marijuana. Your uncle is growing dagga in your garden.

Morgan: Sekuru, that is criminal! It is not allowed by the law to grow *mbanje!*

Dorcas: *(intruding).* People get arrested for possessing *mbanje.* *Mbanje* is a prohibited drug.

Maidei: I have always suspected that weed to be *mbanje.* I could not confront him because I was not sure. *(She walks out.)*

---

18.   Grandson Dzingai
19.   Dagga

70

Mutumwa: That prohibited drug is being grown in your garden. Now, tell me this, Dzingai. If the police were to find out that *mbanje* is growing in your garden, whom do you think they would arrest?

Morgan: The gardener, of course, Sekuru.

Dorcas: Yes, the gardener! He is the one growing *mbanje*.

Mutumwa: *(laughs and sits down).* No, Dzingai. No, Mufaro. *(Dzingai and Dorcas sit down.)* The gardener does not own the garden. The gardener plants what the owner of the garden wants grown there. The police are going to arrest you and your father.

Dorcas: Sekuru, what if our father does not know that the gardener has been growing this *mbanje* in the garden?

Morgan: I am sure my father does not know what is being grown in the garden.

Mutumwa: Why doesn't your father know what is being grown in his garden?

Morgan: Father does not go to the garden.

Mutumwa: Why doesn't your father go to his garden?

Morgan: I do not know why.

Dorcas: *(grabs the plant from Morgan and smells it).* So this is what dagga smells like?

Mutumwa: That is dagga, marijuana! There must be not less than one hundred plants of *mbanje* there growing in plenty of water and fertilizer. When were you last in your garden, Mufaro?

Dorcas: I do not go to the garden. I only see the vegetables when Johannes brings them to the kitchen.

Mutumwa: Who is Johannes?

Dorcas: The gardener.

Mutumwa: Dzingai, correct your sister.

Morgan: *(lecturing to Dorcas).* The gardener is a Madyirapazhe. He is of the Gumbo totem. According to that totem, the gardener is our mother's brother. He is our uncle. He is Sekuru.

Dorcas: *(laughs and waves Morgan off).* Totem . . . *Gumbo* . . . leg . . . *Madyira* . . . . That is crazy.

(Mutumwa stands up, grabs the mbanje plant from Dorcas and walks out showing anger. Morgan and Dorcas are surprised.)

Dorcas: Now what?

Morgan: Sekuru is angry with you.

Dorcas: What have I done?

Morgan: You laughed at Sekuru.

Dorcas: I did not laugh at Sekuru. I laughed at your talk of totems, of legs, of Madyira ....

Morgan: It was not me talking. It was Sekuru talking.

Dorcas: What are you talking about, Morgan? Have you
            become our grandfather?

Morgan: You do not understand Sekuru.

Dorcas: Suddenly, you understand our grandfather. How
            come? You are behaving as if you have just come
            from the village with him and that you are his
            interpreter, his spokesperson, his mouthpiece, his
            medium, his . . . .

Morgan: I do not think that even if I explain you will understand.

Dorcas: I will not understand?

Morgan: No. You will not understand!

*(Morgan puts on his earphones and ignores Dorcas. She removes
the earphones and shouts at him confrontationally.)*

Dorcas: What is it that I will not understand?

Morgan: I do not need to waste my time explaining why you do
            not understand such totems like Sipambi, Nyamuziwa,
            Madyirapazhe, Mhazi, Gurundoro . . . .

Dorcas: *(laughs off Morgan's statement).* Guru. . . what?

Morgan: *(forcefully).* Gurundoro!

Dorcas: Gurundoro? What is that?

Morgan: You will not understand even if I explain. *(He grabs his earphones, puts them on and begins to work on his cellphone. Dorcas laughs, then puts on the earphones and sits down and begins to work on her cellphone. Dorcas laughs to herself. Morgan turns to her. She ignores him and continues laughing. Mutumwa enters carrying a bunch of mbanje leaves. He looks at Dorcas and Morgan who ignore his presence. He sits down and looks at his grandchildren who are busy on their cellphones. Mutumwa puts the bunch of mbanje leaves on the coffee table, stands up and goes to Dorcas and Morgan. He removes their earphones and grabs their cellphones. Morgan is shocked by the action.)*

Morgan: Sekuru, what is wrong? You are taking away our cellphones.

(Mutumwa puts the cellphones in his hat.)

Mutumwa: *(sitting down).* Talk to me!

Dorcas: Talk to you about what, Sekuru?

Mutumwa: Talk to me whatever you want to talk about. Talk to me about your school, yourselves, your friends, your parents and other issues.

Morgan: Sekuru, when we are quiet and working on our cellphones, we are talking to many people, many friends.

74

Dorcas: We are Googling… WhatsApp… twitting … Facebook and….

Mutumwa: Why do you talk to other people and not to me who is here with you?

Dorcas: Because we do not have anything to talk to you about.

Mutumwa: Have you asked me about your grandmother, your father's uncles, your grandmother's sisters and . . .?

Morgan: I do not think we have any questions about them.

Dorcas: Sekuru, do you want to talk to us about them?

Mutumwa: *(shakes his head).* Take your phones. *(Dorcas and Morgan hesitate.)* I said, take your phones! *(Dorcas and Morgan stand up hesitantly and pick up their cellphones, put them on, sit down and begin to work on them. Mutumwa looks at them curiously. A car bell is sounded. Morgan and Dorcas continue working on their cellphones. Maidei enters and rushes to the main entrance and meets Mr. Joseph Matanga and Mrs. Monica Matanga. Maidei takes the briefcase from Joseph and the shopping bag from Monica. Mutumwa stops Maidei.)*

Mutumwa: Give me that shopping bag and the briefcase, Muzukuru! *(Maidei takes the shopping bag and the briefcase to Mutumwa. Mutumwa points to a coffee table. Maidei puts the items on the coffee table.*

Joseph and Monica are surprised. Mutumwa shouts.) Dzingai, leave what you are doing and get your father's briefcase! It should not be Maidei to receive things from your father. You should welcome your father. You, too, Mufaro, get the shopping bag from your mother. That is your responsibility, not of Maidei. *(Morgan and Dorcas walk off being followed by Maidei.)* Stop there! Take off your cellphones. Put them on the coffee table and do not come back until we call for you! *(Dorcas and Morgan take off their cellphones and put them on the coffee table and begin to walk.)* Stop! *(Morgan and Dorcas stop.)* You have not spoken to your parents. Have you been with them the whole day? *(Dorcas and Morgan turn to face their parents.)*

Dorcas: Good evening, Father!

Mutumwa: Mufaro, you are standing in front of your Father!

Dorcas: *(kneels down).* Good evening, Father.

Joseph: Good evening, my daughter.

Morgan: *(crouches).* Good evening, Mother.

Monica: Good evening, my son.

Dorcas: Good evening, Mother!

Monica: Good evening, my daughter. How was your day?

Dorcas: My day was fine.

Morgan: Good evening, Father.

Joseph: Good evening, my son.

(Maidei walks out.)

Mutumwa: *(protesting).* No. Baba Mufaro! Dzingai is not just your son. He is Shumba, Sipambi. I did not hear you call him that!

Joseph: *(excitedly).* How was your day, Shumba?

Morgan: My day was fine, Sipambi.

(Mutumwa, Joseph and Monica laugh. Morgan is confused.)

Mutumwa: Good. Just call him Shumba. Now you can go. Take your phones!

(Dorcas and Morgan take their phones and walk out.)

Joseph: Welcome, Baba. *(He extends a hand for the greeting.)*

Mutumwa: *(shaking his son's hand).* Thank you, Shumba.

Monica: *(rushes to Mutumwa, kneels down and extends her right hand outstretched and a left hand holding the right wrist). Kaziwai* Baba.[20]

Mutumwa: *Mhoro* Muroora![21]

---

20.   Greetings, Father
21.   Greetings, daughter-in-law

Joseph: My sister told me that you had come. *(Mutumwa sits down.)*

Monica: Baba Dorcas, you did not tell me that Baba was here. *(She sits down.)*

Joseph: I was about to tell you when you started accusing me of becoming a slave to golf. *(He sits down near his father.)* How are you Baba?

Mutumwa: I am very well, my son. How are you?

Joseph: I am well, Baba. How is my Mother?

Mutumwa: She is well. She went to a church meeting in Mvuma yesterday.

Monica: *(clapping hands).* How are you, Baba?

Mutumwa: I am very well MaGumbo. How are you?

Monica: I am well, Baba. How is the rest of the family at home?

Mutumwa: They are all well at home. How are the Madyirapazhe here in Harare and in Gutu?

Monica: They are all well. We had a wedding last week. My elder brother's son, Amos, married the daughter of Headmaster Mazhandu of Shurugwi.

Mutumwa: *Makorokoto!*[22]

---

22.   Congratulations!

Monica: Thank you, Sipambi.

Mutumwa: We were not invited!

Joseph: The wedding took place in the United States of America.

Monica: Only my elder sister Tete Munda and my brother and his wife went to America.

Mutumwa: *(picks the plant of mbanje from underneath the coffee table and speaks urgently).* Mai Mufaro, what is this vegetable from your garden?

Monica: A vegetable from our garden?

Mutumwa: It is a vegetable from your garden.

Monica: I have never seen that vegetable in the kitchen. What is it, Baba Dorcas?

Joseph: That plant is *mbanje*, Mai Dorcas.

Monica: *Mbanje*?

Mutumwa: Marijuana.

Monica: It is a crime to grow *mbanje*! People get arrested.

Mutumwa: Yes. You are lucky that none of your neighbours informed the police that your husband is growing *mbanje*.

Joseph: *(protesting).* Baba, I am not growing *mbanje*!

Mutumwa: *(laughs).* Baba Mufaro, who has grown *mbanje* in your garden? Your son Dzingai?

Joseph: I do not think so. He never gets into the garden.

Mutumwa: Is it your daughter Mufaro?

Monica: No. She never gets into the garden.

Mutumwa: Is it you, Mai Mufaro, who is growing *mbanje* in the garden?

Monica: *(laughing).* No. It must be the gardener.

Mutumwa: Johannes, your brother, is growing *mbanje* in your garden?

Monica: Baba, Johannes is not my brother.

Mutumwa: He is a Madyirapazhe... a Gumbo.

Monica: Yes. He is of my totem but not my brother. *(Mutumwa laughs.)* I see. According to totems, he is my brother. He is growing *mbanje* in our garden. He is a criminal. He is. . . .

Mutumwa: *(forcefully).* Your son does not know what is growing in his garden. It seems you also do not know what is growing in your garden because you all eat what you do not grow. *(Monica and Joseph laugh.)* I am not joking. That son of yours does not know what is growing in his garden. What type of a man are you growing?

Joseph: Well, Baba. Morgan has no time for the garden. He is busy with homework when he comes from school. I leave home early in the morning and come back home this late in the evening. I have no time for the garden.

Monica: We all do not have time for the garden. Dorcas has a lot of homework to do when she returns from school. That is why we have employed a gardener and a maid.

Mutumwa: What about Saturday and Sunday? Do you go to work on those days? Do your children go to school on Saturday and Sunday?

Joseph: Baba, working in the garden is not necessary.

Mutumwa: *(laughs).* But you learnt everything about growing food from me. You went to school and had a lot of homework but I made sure that you were in the garden where you grew all types of vegetables which you sold to your teachers. When you were twelve, you grew carrots which your teacher considered the best carrots he had ever eaten. You grew maize. You grew cucumbers. You grew watermelons. You grew. . . .

Joseph: *(laughing).* Baba, times have changed. We do not need to sell vegetables to send these children to school. I am a well-paid government accountant. She runs a very successful preschool business. These children do not need to bother about growing anything in that garden. We provide for all their needs. *(Mutumwa laughs. Joseph is surprised and offended.)* Father, I am not joking!

Mutumwa: And you are happy to grow children who are handi-capped?

Monica: Handicapped? You are saying that our children are handicapped?

Mutumwa: Yes. They are disabled. Totally handicapped mentally and physically. They cannot do anything in this house. Your daughter is handicapped. She does not even know how to serve me tea. *(Monica and Joseph laugh. Mutumwa shouts harshly.)* I am not joking! These children are disabled. They have not grown up. They are babies. They know nothing about our family and what is expected of them. You do not talk to them. They only know what they read in books and what teachers tell them. They do not benefit from you as father and mother. In fact, they are orphans.

Joseph: *(getting angry).* Orphans? Father! You are mixing up things. You are stuck in the olden days of doing things. You do not stay here. You do not know what happens here. I provide my children with everything they need. They do not have to work the way I did. *(Enthusiastically and angrily.)* You woke us up at 4am to go and work in the maize field. At 6am, we milked the cows, then washed with cold water from the dam. We did not eat breakfast but carried *mutakura*[23] to school and walked seven kilometres to school. We came back from school eating our

_____

23. A dish of boiled maize mixed with peanuts or cow peas.

mutakura as our lunch, took off our uniforms and went straight to the fields to weed or harvest the crops until 7pm. *(Mutumwa laughs.)* Father, we worked like slaves. By the time I was in Grade Seven, I had done everything expected of a man. Everything! Yoking oxen, sowing and weeding the crops, making compost manure, making hoe and axe handles, and even cutting down trees and producing yokes, stools and benches. I never grew up as a child. I never. . . .

Mutumwa: My son, please shut up! *(Monica holds her husband's hand to comfort him and helps him to keep quiet.)* You worked like a slave in our fields for us to grow crops to sell and get money for your school fees, your shoes, your books. You worked for everything you needed for your education and your stomach. You worked in your fields. You looked after your cattle and even read your books while looking after your cattle. We sold the cattle to get money for boarding fees. And yet you were always number one in class until you went to boarding school and did well to get to university and still came back home on holidays to work in the fields.

Joseph: I was number one in school because I was intelligent! *(Mutumwa and Monica laugh. Joseph is surprised.)* Yes, I was brilliant. I read all books thoroughly. *(Mutumwa and Monica continue to laugh.)*

Monica: No, Baba Dorcas. You are missing Baba's point. Working in the fields did not stop you from performing well in school. Working in the fields made you a man that I know and love. When we got married, you worked in our garden and made many items that are in this house. You made the cooking sticks I used. You did not want me to buy things you could make with your hands. *(Joseph begins to laugh.)* You even thought that you could teach me how to iron your own clothes. *(Joseph laughs again.)* We bought this house because you wanted a big garden. You wanted to grow all the things you used to grow at home and which your father taught you to grow. *(Mutumwa claps his hands and whistles loudly. Joseph joins in clapping hands. Monica is excited and laughs. They all laugh.)*

Joseph: *(shouts).* Go on, Mai Dorcas! Remind me. (*Monica and Mutumwa laugh heartily.*)

Monica: You told my younger sister that my kitchen was her laboratory. When she went to America she wrote back saying that she was practising what you and I taught her in that kitchen. You were even able to teach me how to cook *rupiza*,[24] how to cook *nhopi*[25] and *maqebelengwane*.[26]

Joseph: *(laughs).* We used to call that baked *sadza* with sugar, *chifuturamvana*.[27] *(They all laugh.)*

---

24.   A dish of roasted and grounded cow peas, then cooked as porridge.
25.   Rich food of mashed pumpkin mixed with peanut butter, brown granulated sugar and a pinch of salt.
26.   Sugared maize meal lumps
27.   Food that fattens single mothers

Monica: It was not baked *sadza*, but a cake made of maize flour with sugar!

Joseph: Yes. You are right. I even taught you how to fry flying ants, *ishwa!*

Monica: *(laughing).* Yes. And how to fry the big-bellied black flying ants, *sambarafuta.*

Joseph: Yes, *sambarafuta*! *(Laughs.)* But I could not teach you how to eat unfried *sambarafuta.*

Monica: Argh! *(Laughing.)* Baba, your son could catch the big-bellied black flying ants as they emerged from their holes in anthills, take off their wings and throw the insects into his mouth, chew them and swallow. Argh! *(Joseph laughs. Mutumwa laughs.)* It was really disgusting!

Mutumwa: They learnt to do that when they were looking after cattle in the bush.

Joseph: *(pompously).* We made instant sour milk in the bush.

Monica: No, that is not possible. Instant sour milk?

Mutumwa. Yes, they did that.

Joseph: We milked the cows, then put a certain fruit into the milk. . . .

Mutumwa: *Nhengeni!*[28]

---

28.   A type of wild fruit

Joseph: Yes, *nhengeni*. The unripe *nhengeni* fruits were like lemons. We put the juice of *nhengeni* into the fresh milk and in a matter of minutes it became sour milk that we enjoyed as lunch.

Mutumwa: Yes. We knew that you were milking the cows in the bush because, one day, you came home with a swollen eye.

(Joseph laughs.)

Monica: What had happened?

Joseph: I always milked our favourite cow, Juliet, without tying its legs. But, one day, when I was milking her as usual, she kicked me on the eye, the right eye. It was because we had removed its calf from the milk too soon.

Monica: *(shocked and covering her eyes with her hands).* It kicked your eye?

Joseph: Yes.

Mutumwa: The wound was terrible! We feared that he would lose his eye. We were lucky that Dr. Mutemeri attended to your husband the following day. He made sure that the eye was totally healed.

Monica: Where is Dr Mutemeri now? I want to go and thank him for saving my husband's eye. *(They all laugh.)* He would have become blind or one-eyed. He would not have been academically successful to become a top civil servant. I do not think I would have been attracted to a one-eyed man. *(Joseph and Monica laugh.)*

Joseph: Baba, you were right. We grew up learning how to use our hands and our minds to survive. By the time we were thirteen years old, we could do almost everything that can sustain one in life. We became independent at thirteen. We were self-sufficient and always resourceful. I am sorry that I have not played my role as a father to Morgan. I am going to try hard to correct that mistake.

Monica: I am sorry Baba for not helping Dorcas to know how to cook. It is wrong to justify our actions by saying that we provide our children with everything they need. What could happen if both of us were suddenly not able to work? An accident could cripple both of us. We have no excuse. When my mother visited us, Dorcas could not even cook rice with peanut butter. She simply put peanut butter into the rice. My mother scolded me for that. She was furious. She said that I had turned my maid into the mother of my daughter. I cried. I never told Baba Dorcas what my mother said.

Joseph: She was here last week, Mai Dorcas. Why did you not tell me that your mother was disappointed with you?

Monica: *(confronting her husband).* What would you have done? My mother was also disappointed with you.

Joseph: *(angrily).* Disappointed with me?

Monica: *(angrily).* Yes. You thanked her with my totem. She is not Madyirapazhe. She is Shava Museyamwa.

Mutumwa: *(angrily).* Joseph, how could you insult your mother-in-law by indicating that her husband was her brother?

Joseph: For goodness, Father, it was just a mistake. Anyone can make such a mistake.

Monica: *(angrily).* No! Not anyone but an absent-minded husband! My mother accused me of not telling you her totem and for not teaching you how to thank her.

Joseph: *(agitated).* We have not lived for any substantial time with your mother here. She always goes to your brothers.

Monica: Why? Why does she go to my brothers? *(Even more emotional.)* How could she be comfortable staying in a house where the head of the house does not know how to. . . .

Joseph: *(shouting).* Okay! I am sorry. I am very sorry!

Monica: *(emotional).* You do not have to apologise to me but to my mother.

Joseph: *(equally emotional).* Apologise?

Mutumwa: *(calming the tempers).* Yes, Shumba. You will have to say to her, "Sorry for saying Gumbo Madyirapazhe. I should have said, *(Clapping.)* '*Maita* Shava. *Ziwewera. Hekani Mutekedza. Vakatekedzana paJanga.*[29] *(Monica ululates.)*' Then you give your mother-in-law a goat and plead for forgiveness for insulting her.

Joseph: A goat?

Mutumwa: *(calming the tempers).* You are lucky that your mother-in-law comes from Zvimba. If she were from Gutu, you would pay a cow.

Joseph: A cow? Just for that small mistake?

Monica: Baba. I am sorry, your son has a lot to learn about our culture.

Mutumwa: Muroora. Please, do not blame me. Blame his boarding school, KwaTsambe, St. Augustine Mission. From Form Three up to Form Six, he stayed with Father Stanley at St. Augustine's during the holidays, working in the school's accounts department. He did not come home for many years. Even when he was at the University of Zimbabwe, he worked at Mr. Gumbo's shop, here in Harare, doing his accounts. When he told his mother's brothers that he wanted to marry you, they had to make sure that he had a crash course on our customs and traditions before coming to your parents to ask for your hand in marriage.

---

29.   Thank you, Eland. Great visible one. Behold the honoured one. One honoured one at Janga.

Monica: *(laughing).* A crash course in our culture?

Joseph: Yes. *(Laughs.)* Two months of heritage studies. It was hard. *(Mutumwa laughs.)* I had to pay my uncles to teach me about what the people of Zvimba do in marriage negotiations. All the things about paying *roora* for the time the woman you are to marry was touching and playing with her father's beard when she was a baby.

Mutumwa: *(laughing). Matekenyandebvu!*[30] *(Monica laughs.)*

Joseph: And the. . . .

Mutumwa: *(laughing).* All the things we do not do in Gutu.

Joseph: Such as paying *roora* for the cloth that tied the mother's womb that was carrying the woman you want to marry! *(Monica and Mutumwa laugh. Joseph joins them in laughing.)*

Mutumwa: *(laughing).* When we were at the *roora* negotiations, we did not realise your father's family were from Gutu, Gumbo Madyirapazhe who had settled in Zvimba in 1950.

Joseph: They did not belong to the Zvimba people. They used the marriage customs of the area to get us to pay *roora* for many issues which we did not think should be included in. . . .

---

30.   Playing with father's beard when the child was a baby.

Monica: *(interrupting to stop).* You have not finished paying the *roora*, my husband!

Joseph: *(light-heartedly).* Nobody in his right mind can finish paying *roora*. Your father's brother asked for a kraal of 15 head of cattle!

(Monica laughs. Mutumwa and Joseph join in the laughter. They all stop laughing when Dorcas enters with a tray with tea. She is accompanied by Maidei who is carrying a dish of water and a towel, and Morgan who is carrying newspapers and magazines. Joseph, Mutumwa and Monica are surprised. Dorcas kneels down and puts the tray on the coffee table. She removes the embroidery covering the tray with tea, claps hands and speaks confidently to her father.)

Dorcas: *(clapping hands).* Shumba, this is your tea that I have prepared. I request that my mother, VaMagumbo, Madyirapazhe, joins you. My husband, Sekuru here, has just had his tea with bread and jam. *(Mutumwa claps hands. Joseph is excited and he joins in clapping hands. Monica joins them in clapping hands. Dorcas smiles victoriously. Morgan crouches before his father. Claps hands.)* Sipambi, these are newspapers and magazines that came for you. My sister and I have already learnt a lot from Grandfather. We are delighted he is here.

Monica: *(excitedly).* We are going to learn a lot more from him in the three weeks he is going to be with us.

Morgan: Excuse, Baba. Excuse me, Sekuru. Excuse, *Amai*.[31] I have an important announcement to make.

Joseph: Go ahead, my son.

Morgan: Sekuru!

Mutumwa: Go ahead, Muzukuru!

Morgan: Mother!

Monica: Go ahead, my son, but please do not shock us.

Morgan: *(announcing like an adult).* My name is Dzingai Morgan Matanga, Shumba, Sipambi! When you are not here, Dad, I am the head of this family and this household. I promise to be very responsible.

(Mutumwa claps his hands. Joseph joins clapping hands. Monica ululates and she is joined by Maidei. Mutumwa stands up and shouts.)

Mutumwa: We have heard you, Shumba!. *Maita* Shumba! *Zvaitwa* Sipambi! *(To Joseph.)* My son, this announcement calls for a celebration. A *bira* for thanksgiving. Do you have drums in this house?

Joseph: Unfortunately, we do not have drums here.

Mutumwa: What about *hosho*?[32]

---

31.   Mother
32.   Rattles

Monica: I am the only one with *hosho*, but I left them at the church.

Maidei: The gardener has drums.

Mutumwa: *(with urgency).* Muzukuru, go and get Madyira and his drums! Do not explain anything to him. Tell him that he is wanted urgently with his drums by the father of his boss.

Maidei: I will do that, Shumba. He knows that you are here. *(Maidei rushes out.)*

Mutumwa: Now, what songs shall we sing? Mufaro, what songs shall we sing for the *bira* of thanksgiving.

Dorcas: I do not know any songs, Sekuru. What is *bira*?

Mutumwa: Bira is a prayer to God, *Musikavanhu*,[33] through our ancestors.

Morgan: *(with urgency).* But Sekuru, what dance shall we perform? That will tell us what songs we can sing.

Mutumwa: Good question, Dzingai. Good question. We can dance *mhande*.[34]

Morgan: *(confidently).* I know the songs for *mhande*.

Joseph: You know the songs?

---

33.   Creator of the people/humanity
34.   A type of traditional dance

Morgan: Yes. I know the songs and can dance *mhande*.

Mutumwa: Good. Very good. Everything is here for the *bira*.

Joseph: *(inquisitively).* Where did you learn the song, Morgan?

Morgan: I was a member of CHIPAWO Traditional Dance Group for two terms before I joined the Jibilika Hip-hop Dance Group.

Monica: *(shouts with excitement).* Oh, yes. I gave you the money for membership to those clubs.

Morgan: Yes, Mother. Thank you.

Mutumwa: *(excitedly).* If you know *mhande*, then you know the dance for *bira*. We can also do the *mbira* dance.

Morgan: I know songs such as *(Singing.) Dzinomwa muna Save. Mhondoro dzinomwa.*[35] *(Mutumwa joins in the singing and clapping hands. Joseph, Monica and Dorcas watch them unsure of what to do. Maidei enters carrying hosho and is followed by Johannes who is carrying a drum.)*

Mutumwa: *(shouts).* Come in Sekuru Madyira! Welcome to our *bira* of thanksgiving! *(Johannes smiles happily.)* Move the sofas to create room for the *bira*. *(Joseph and Morgan move the sofas.)* Madyira, play us the drum for *mhande*.

---

35.   They drink from Save River. The Lion spirits drink.

Johannes: Yes, Sekuru! *(Plays the mhande drum.)*

Mutumwa: *(stops Johannes).* That is good Madyirapazhe.. *Vaidyira pazhe nokutya vayeraShiri.[36] (Johannes laughs heartily.)* Gumbo that is *mhande!* Now, Muzukuru Dzingai, pick my walking stick. *(Morgan picks up the walking stick and goes with it to Mutumwa.)* Hold it, Muzukuru. It is yours for now. You are now my father Dzingai. We celebrate your being here. *(He picks up his hat.)* Now put this hat on. *(Morgan smiles and puts the hat on. Mutumwa begins to sing pointing at Morgan.) Dzingai ndibaba! Tavavona havo ndibaba vedu. Tavavona netsvimbo yavo![37] (Johannes and Maidei join in the singing. Johannes plays the drum singing. Maidei plays hosho. Joseph joins in the singing. Dorcas is struggling with the handclapping. Her mother joins in the singing and clapping. Mutumwa takes to the floor and dances facing Morgan who joins him and dances. Maidei ululates. Monica joins in the ululating and leads the song. Mutumwa leaves Morgan who is dancing some variations of the mhande dance. His mother ululates and joins in the dance. Mutumwa signals Johannes to stop drums and continues to clap as Morgan stops dances. Monica and Maidei ululate. Dorcas joins them*

---

36. Those who ate meals sitting outside because of fearing the invading Hungwe (type of bird) people.
37. We have seen him, he is our father. We have seen him with his walking stick.

as Mutumwa takes Morgan and gets him to sit on the sofa. He crouches on the ground and begins clapping hands to Morgan. Johannes and Joseph follow suit. Maidei leads Monica and Dorcas to kneel as they ululate and join in the clapping.)

Mutumwa: *(recites the Shumba Sipambi totemic praise).*

Maita Shumba.
Zvaitwa Sipambi.
Yakapamba nedzavamwe.
Vadyi vevhazhakamwe.
Inodyarwa ikamera.
Matikaha nekuona tsimba.
Kuona munhu vana votya.
Kumuka ndodzvova.
Kutsika zvovava.
Mukarakatirwa kwasviba.
Mutakuranhowo kuno munhuwi.
Sipambi mwana wechikara.

---

38. Thank you, Lion
     It is done, Sipambi (the Grabber).
     The eaters of the seed that is boiled for few moments and remains uncooked.
     When it passes through the digestive system it still germinates if it is planted.
     Surprised mainly by the sight of its footprints.
     When it looks at people, children get scared.
     Waking up, I roar.
     Stalking as if the ground is hot.
     The senser of the scent of potential prey.
     Sipambi, the child of the beast.

Chokanyaira chobva Magare.
Choinda imbwarume chisina uta.
Mazvita vari Dinhire chigarachibwe.
Vari Magare VaMupfurawatya.
Mazviita mugonderwa vokwaMusakadongo.
VeShange vari Mudzimudzangara.
Vari Sikanadema.

Zvaitwa vatakaindisa naMuzuva.
Vari Ruvhure.
Waita Charumbira.
Zvigonyati zvangu zvizvi.
Haiwa zvaitwa vaNhinhi vari Nhinhihuru.
Maita Saminzwa.
Vari Nyanda.[38]

Proudly stepping out of its den at Magare.
Wild dog goes for hunting without weapons
Thank you those who lie at Dinhire, the stone where the lion sits.
Those buried at Magare, whom many fought with fear.
Thank you the great strategist in hunting, those of Musakadongo.
Those of Shange in Mudzimudzangara (the feared shadows).
Those buried in Sikanadema (the place of dark complexion girls)
It has been done, those we sent with Muzuva.
Those who lie at Ruvhure.
You have done well Charumbira (the praised one).
It has been done, the tough ones who lie at the place of tough ones.
Well done survivor in the middle of unpleasant bushes.
Those who lie at Nyanda.

(He claps his hands. Maidei ululates. Monica joins in the ululation. Morgan beams with a big smile. Mutumwa stands up and goes to Morgan and extends his hand for a handshake. Morgan grabs it enthusiastically, standing up. Mutumwa takes back his walking stick and his hat. Joseph extends his hand which his son grabs.)

Joseph: *Maita* Shumba!

Monica: *(comes forward and shakes her son's hand).* Maita Sipambi!

(Maidei pushes Dorcas forward. She is not forthcoming. Morgan walks to his sister and holds her hand.)

Morgan: *(shouting).* Thank you, MaSibanda, *(Maidei ululates. Monica ululates. Dorcas laughs and covers her face laughing. Morgan goes to Johannes and extends his hand shouting.)* Thank you, Sekuru!

Johannes: *(enthusiastically).* Thank you, Shumba!

Maidei: *(starts a celebration song).* Nhasi ndezvedu![39] Taitambira zvavamwe.[40] *(She is joined by all who conclude by clapping hands, ululation and whistles.)*

---

39.   Today, we celebrate our success!
40.   In the past, we used to take part in celebrating others' success.

Printed in the United States
By Bookmasters